THE NEW SALES LEADER

HOW TO TRANSFORM THE SALES TEAM WITH THE TRUSTED ADVISOR SELLING METHOD

Brad Tonini

TRUSTED
ADVISOR
PRESS

1213/1 Queens Road, Melbourne, Australia
brad@bradtonini.com

ISBN: 978-0-6489112-3-4 PAPERBACK
ISBN: 978-0-6489112-4-1 HARDBACK

Cover and interior design *LRB Publishing Services*
contact@lindaruthbrooks.com
Nonfiction/sales education/

THE NEW SALES LEADER is a sales instruction manual, designed to assist salespersons of all areas to gain valuable information on ways to optimise sales opportunities through presentation, high standard behaviour and becoming trusted advisors to their clients. Every attempt has been made to give appropriate acknowledgment for material, visual or written.

THE NEW SALES LEADER

HOW TO TRANSFORM THE SALES TEAM WITH THE TRUSTED ADVISOR SELLING METHOD

BRAD TONINI

Dedication page

To my family who are always there to cheer me on in the game of life … thank you!

To the salespeople who every day put themselves out there … be proud of the greatest profession!

To the sales managers who juggle the selling efforts of the organisation, who sometimes feel lonely and need to come up with the answers, and who aspire to be the dynamic sales leader, I salute you!

Contents

Other titles by Brad Tonini:

Time for Life

Make it Happen Now!

The New Rules of the Game

101 Ways to Keep the Sales Focus

Sales 101

7 Keys to Presenting Ideas That Sell

The Great Theatre of the Sale

INTRODUCTION

The life of a sales manager can be a lonely one.

Day to day you feel you need to look like you have the answers for the sales team, even though there are no guarantees that everything you are suggesting to do will work.

You have a Managing Director or CEO above you who wants answers—"Why aren't we reaching our sales budget?" I can hear them saying.

They may have never been in selling themselves and may have come from finance or manufacturing. They believe sales is just sales—nothing different from any of the other middle management functions.

It's hard to find someone to talk to, to confide in.

I guess that's where I make my living. For over 15 years, I have been a sounding board and trusted advisor to many of you, and I love the journey.

Once we get past the chest beating and putting on the show for the MD and we are sitting there one on one and discussing real issues, we make a connection.

You see, the sales manager gets the blame for a lot of things—whether it be the sales budget not being achieved or the customer service department having to save the day through the actions of a "rogue" salesperson who has promised something you can't possibly deliver, you get drawn into it all.

The warehouse manager may even be at your doorway throwing up their hands in despair due to the impatient salesperson standing over them asking when their urgent order can be despatched.

It can be the best of times and the worst of times.

I am one of you—or at least I was for a number of years before I entered the world of consulting and professional speaking.

I had my own international business in the stationery business selling executive diaries, organisers, promotional products, pretty much anything you could pop a logo onto.

My sales team consisted of a field sales team of five, two telemarketers, and then a group of agents who would represent my brand across Australia, New Zealand, and the Pacific Islands.

Not a massive team, but when you are running a business with no dedicated sales manager, I was busy.

I seemed to always be in a tug of war with everyone, trying to keep the customer happy while making sure that every salesperson on the team was in alignment with my philosophy. I tried too hard to make everyone happy, and I thought I had to have all the answers, when in reality I didn't.

Today, a little more vulnerability and perhaps a more "consultative style" works to your advantage, as long as you are not trying to accommodate everyone.

In my time, being more transparent and open about the numbers and the latest information about the stock movements from Asia (which is something that my salespeople were always asking for) would have been paramount in building trust with the sales team and getting the answers out at the coal face.

Sales managers need to have more strategic skills and more emotional intelligence today, similar to being an AFL coach where you get the team humming by understanding each of the team members well and knowing which buttons to press.

I think the old role of the sales manager is now obsolete and, I will talk about that in the next chapter.

The sales leader is the new and different breed—they are focused on transforming the sales team into a dynamic, motivated, and focused sales force.

It requires us to create new processes and structures that the team can follow consistently. But at the same time, we need to make tweaks to the structures if there is a better way.

Transformation also requires you to invest in yourself to be a better leader of people and to learn or "re-tool" when the market requires it.

"How many times do I have to tell the guys about our unique advantage, our pricing, our specials for the month, the product features and benefits?" I can hear myself saying over and over again.

We call this the "blame game," where it's their fault for not achieving the numbers each month. Perhaps it's easier for us to report it back to the CEO that way?

I didn't promise that this book was going to be a nice "soft read." I don't think you would be interested in reading on if it was, to be honest.

The hundreds of sales managers (responsible for thousands of salespeople) I have worked with one to one over the last 15 years never liked me dressing anything up: "Just tell me what I should do" was usually the mantra in our sessions. So that's the approach I have taken in writing this book.

The journey you are about to go on is one that talks about the new buyer and what they now need; it will give you an opportunity to review your own team and identify where you need to re-tool skills.

It will also provide you a pathway to success broken up into three areas: transformational thinking, transformational systems, and transformational coaching.

Enjoy the process, grab a pen, and feel free to write all over the book when something makes sense to you (I do when I read any business book), and then use the book as a toolbox with some practical ideas you can keep referring to .

I wish you well and I really hope our paths may cross if I don't already know you—to share a few war stories and to talk about how sales leadership can be the most rewarding journey you can go on!

CHAPTER 1

Why Being a Sales Manager Just Isn't Enough

Sales management is not easy, and sales leadership even more demanding. The sales world is changing before us—the challenges of our team are different perhaps to when we were full-time salespeople.

The old sales manager running the team from behind their desk, barking out orders, and jumping up and down at sales meetings is fast disappearing.

So what's required of the new sales leader to make you current and relevant for these times?

Today I have found that there is a significant difference between the sales manager and the sales leader.

Sales Manager vs. Sales Leader

The **sales manager** is reactive to the day and the demands of the sales team; the **sales leader** is proactive and foresees the challenges before they happen.

The **sales manager** gets caught up the day to day or even hour to hour; the **sales leader** is always planning ahead, thinking of next month, the next promotion, the next vertical market.

The **sales manager** constantly wears the backpack and goes out and creates their own results due to the shortfalls in the sales team numbers; the **sales leader** will coach to ensure the sales team gets the numbers.

The **sales manager** will blame the sales team when things are not going to plan; the **sales leader** will ask themselves what they could have done better before looking for the answers inside the team.

The **sales manager** will spend 80 percent of their time on the high maintenance members of their team who don't help themselves; the **sales leader** will direct their energy to those who are coachable.

Sales leadership has come a long way, but it still has a long way to go. Perhaps you can see someone in these avatars who reminds you of the sales manager you had, or maybe, from time to time, you exhibit some of these qualities?

In days gone the typical sales manager was usually one of a number of typical avatars:

The Intimidator:

Perhaps as a sales professional, you had a sales manager who had this style?

Very old style sales management—the type of sales manager who would walk into the sales meeting and on cue drop their folder on the table and start ranting in front of the team about their lack of performance, their lack of effort, and poor attitude.

Calling them names, pointing the finger at individuals, and making them feel small in front of the group. The assumption was that you know what to do, so just do it!

The only problem with this style is it was all fear-based—scare them enough into action and they will perform!

They were the same sales managers who would constantly say to the business owner, "I just can't find any good salespeople out there, they are all hopeless!"

The Motivator:

This style of sales manager was usually a top sales professional who became the sales manager, either based on tenure of years or because they will "show the salespeople how to sell, I did it and so can they."

If you have ever seen the movie *Glengarry Glen Ross* about commission sales timeshare salespeople, you will recognise the character that Alec Baldwin plays as the sales guru. The lead salesperson who comes from head office to the field office to rant to the underperforming sales team sharing stories about how they could do it!

The only problem with this style of sales manager is that they soon realise the skills they possessed to be a great salesperson are not the same ones required to be a great sales leader.

They may have known how to sell, but they are not capable of showing and teaching others. They get frustrated and then go outside the team and start to try to achieve the sales budget on their own.

The motivator can give the sales team a good motivational speech at the weekly sales meeting and show motivational videos to get them fired up. That works for about one hour after the meeting and then the sales professionals come down after their sugar rush and struggle to maintain the rage.

No supportive coaching and processes developed to help the sales team soon turns into the sales manager talking louder and louder and looking for new recruits out in the market that are more like them. Now you have a whole team without any processes or structures but plenty of passion.

The Administrator:

When a sales manager is placed in front of the team with very little field sales experience or from an administration background, the sales team finds it hard to respect their role.

The sales team wants someone who "gets it," who understands what it's like to get more "no's" than "yes's" whilst out there prospecting and pitching for new business.

The administrator is great at producing reports, putting together sales graphs, and talking about what has happened in the business, but doesn't have the answers to a game plan to break new ground in the market.

They are more of a support to the sales team; nice person, but they feel intimidated by the sales team as they know they don't have the same level of experience as some of the crusty old salespeople on the sales team.

They spend a good deal of their time really being the sales coordinator—following up on sales requests, orders that are running late, special pricing, and the status of stock arriving from overseas.

The new sales leader is the **head coach.**

The Head Coach:

The head coach understands that sales success comes from working through the sales team and not trying to carry all the responsibility of sales success in the organisation by themselves.

They understand that everyone is different and needs their own individual performance plan, and they know they need to invest in each of the salespeople individually to find and play to their hot buttons.

The head coach enlists the help of others, doesn't profess to have all the answers, but has a strong desire to find out what they might be. They are curious—they build in their mind the perfect sales professional model and work with the team to try and play to each person's strengths.

Modelling of great selling by taking parts of each salesperson and deconstructing the makeup a great salesperson in front the team is fundamental to their success.

Here are five things I begin most of my coaching work with sales leaders to lay the foundations to better understand the thinking that goes into being a head coach:

Salespeople think differently from sales managers and business owners. If they thought the same way as us, they would be in business for themselves or running their own team. They have their own view of the world and that's okay.

Each salesperson is a "snowflake," there are no two salespeople that are the same.

Some are motivated by money, some want to be acknowledged, and some want the awards and accolades.

There is no one type.

They are all people and they arrive at our care for different reasons.

Whether you think you have or haven't, every sales team has a sales culture.

Every sales team creates their own environment and rules of engagement; there is a culture present, whether it's the positive proactive culture you are striving for or not is up to you!

To change behaviours in the sales team, you need to have a process and stay the course.

One rant at the weekly sales meeting won't change behaviours for long.

They may leave the room with a clear focus for that day, but without ongoing messaging and coaching, you won't get the change you are looking for.

We always need to be giving clear and explicit instructions and never assuming they just know!

We assume way too much in sales leadership. We assume that they know what process you want them to follow, the way you want them to spend their time, etc.

Ask them to feed back their understanding to you—there is no shortcut!

No formal education

I think the gap in understanding what the true role of the sales leader is starts with the lack of formal education to be a sales leader in the first place. I can't remember there being a university degree on it— and yet it is a critical function.

We learn what the sales manager looks like from other sales managers we have served under—the problem just multiplies.

Most sales managers I have worked with have never been introduced to a strategic sales plan or role played a coaching session with an experienced sales leader to hone their craft.

They learn on the run—perhaps it has a lot to do with sales being the "ugly duckling" to marketing a good deal of the time. Plenty of degrees available for marketing but try finding a degree with a sales stream.

Given this lack of education, there are plenty of misconceptions of sales management, some from inside the profession and some from outside.

Misconceptions of Sales Management

Perhaps you're new to managing the sales team as a sales manager or you are the managing director of your own company. In my years working with sales managers, there are a number of things I have observed as **untruths** in our field:

> ***Being a great salesperson will ensure you make a great sales manager.***

Wrong! The skills required are very different.

You may have been the best performer for months or years in a row, but now that gets put to the side as you are charged with the responsibility to work through your team.

No longer can you be the person to rescue the sales team by putting on the backpack and closing more business. It's now a much bigger job with a much bigger budget.

Commit to a new set of skills required, a different way to think, and a coaching mindset and way of life and you will succeed in building a great sales team.

The most senior in service should get the role

If you are a business owner and you are looking to promote someone to sales manager so you can focus on running and developing the business, be careful to not just promote the person who has been there the longest. Loyalty is one thing, but they also won't necessarily make a great sales manager.

Seniority just means that you have seen a lot and perhaps been a great salesperson over the years.

It doesn't mean that you know what it takes to understand what makes each person tick, to develop a great plan of attack for the team, to market the company correctly, or to lead with consistency and clarity.

You are there to serve the sales team.

As much as you might think so from time to time, your job is not to just offer up special pricing and expedite orders on behalf of the sales team; it's more than that.

You need to be the person who is at the pointy end of the business, guiding the team, showing them the behaviours you are looking for, and being the "go between" with stakeholders in the business and the team out there at the coal face.

Experienced salespeople don't need micro-managing.

I agree that we don't need to be over their shoulder all the time, but a great sales leader takes an active interest in the sales team's development.

Experienced salespeople are not all good learners—they can certainly be the most challenging for the sales trainer or speaker at the conference. Some believe there is nothing new in sales and you are wasting their time by having them off the road for this time. They should not be exempt from the learning pathway, to constantly upskill and to have their results questioned if the numbers just aren't there.

Experienced salespeople don't need a long induction.

Most sales managers with whom I have worked with don't map out a really comprehensive sales induction program.

It's marginally better today from when I started working with sales managers 17 years ago when the Yellow Pages plus the car keys were the extent of the induction program.

Professional salespeople really now expect to know exactly what the expectations are, to get solid product knowledge, and to learn how things are done around here!

But it doesn't stop there—after the initial induction, which should be sales and company-wide, there is ongoing coaching and mentoring.

And… so many sales managers wonder why their recruitment process is like a revolving door!

So given these misconceptions, what does it take to make the grade for the new sales leader in the 2020s and beyond?

Strap yourself in, grab a pen, and get ready.

CHAPTER 2:

The New Sales Leader - The Skills Required and the Questions You Need to be Able to Answer

Whether you are an experienced sales manager or a business owner in a leaner structure with a couple of salespeople, the rules we talk about in this book will help you to be the sales leader required in the 2020s and beyond.

So, what are things that we need to aware of and what skills do we need to focus on to succeed in this new selling world?

Today's buyers want our salespeople to be more responsive, to be experts in the industry, to do what they say they will.

There is a shift in the way our salespeople need to sell—from selling to being of service to our clients first before we have earned the right to ask for their business.

Sure, we all understand the need to make the sales budget and beyond, that goes without saying.

But it's in the method that we need to instruct our salespeople so they can be effective, that's what's changed.

A tighter economy means that buyers can be more risk averse, meaning that we need patient salespeople on our teams who are able to nurture the opportunity without losing their temper, to be able see things from the buyers' point of view.

Think Bigger, Bigger, Bigger

Too many sales managers don't think big enough.

They add a little more on top of the previous year and that makes the next year's budget.

So what is really possible?

Is there a market segment you haven't fully exhausted?

How about a new supply arrangement that might give you an edge in creating organic growth back to your existing base?

As a sales leader, we have to look at everything—the market, the product innovation, the sales team, the ordering cycle, trends in conversion rates, new alliance opportunities, then go back to the drawing board and be bold with predictions.

What sales culture do you want?

This is a really fundamental question to ask as the sales leader sets the tone for the selling efforts, makes the performance standards and not-negotiables clear for the team.

How about your style of leadership required?

Do you need to transition now to be more effective as the macro-manager and not riding the salespeople so tightly but trusting the small day-to-day events and looking more at how you can steer the ship to bigger things?

That's sales leadership.

We are in the business of sales team transformation—to constantly challenge ourselves to find a better way, to fully embrace the potential.

3 Core Transformational Areas Required

Transforming the sales team requires three things: transformational **thinking**, transformational **processes**, and transformational **coaching**.

Transforming the Sales Team

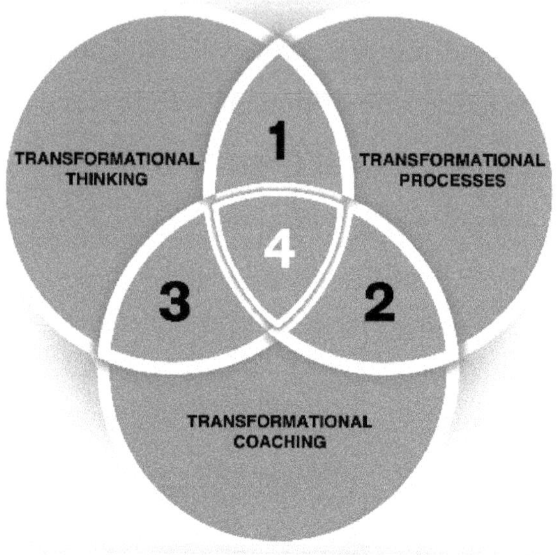

Transforming Your Thinking

By changing our thinking, we take on the mindset of the sales leader. We are proactive, strategically thinking of where the business will be at in three to five years and not just next month.

We are thinking multiple moves ahead of our opposite number and positioning the business not just for strong organic growth but also acquisition opportunities of new accounts.

We have a game plan and we ask our salespeople to be trusted advisors thinking the same way.

Transforming Your Processes

Once we have the thinking right, how do we bed down the roadmap for success?

The sales leader doesn't leave the sales professionals wondering what to do next; they help and align the thinking into models, plans, and processes which provide a framework into how we are going to achieve the big goals of the business.

Transforming Your Coaching

Coaching the team to success is the next part of the journey to set the expectations and have the team buy into the day-to-day habits required then to coach and mentor to success.

The sales leader gets their hands dirty—they know the benefit of leading by example and showing the team how to execute the strategy on each and every sales call.

I started my working life as a tennis coach teaching young "would be" John McEnroes in the bayside suburbs how to swing the perfect forehand. They wanted to improve and they wanted it quickly.

As a tennis coach to young kids for a couple of years while studying at university, I realized pretty quickly you can't tennis coach from the stand. You need to get down on the court with your charger to show and instruct. The same with sales.

Start with These 17 Questions

I use these **17 questions** in my workshops to get the Sales managers to think about where they are on the transition to sales leadership.

Take a look—identify where you need to place your energy-

1: Is your communication uncomplicated, unambiguous and understood by the sales team?

Are you constantly changing priorities with the team and sending mixed messages?

Do you have weekly pet projects that really don't align with the overall plan?

2: Are you riding along with your sales team?

Conducting ride-alongs with your sales team is paramount to checking and observing the quality of the sales process and how they are interacting with the customers.

Rather than assuming they are selling the way you want them to, do you spot check?

3: Are you using the spotlight-floodlight method to coach?

Sales leadership is about observing.

Spotlight in the field with the salesperson, give direct feedback in the car going back to the office, then **floodlight** to the overall sales team at the meeting so the entire sales team gets the benefit of the idea exchange.

4: Are you holding 15-minute power coaching sessions with each salesperson individually?

To get the edge in the team, we must allow 15 minutes per salesperson per week at a minimum to discuss challenges, to sharpen the saw on process, and to win more business.

5: Are you leading and exhibiting the execution of the desired sales process?

We must be showing the sales team what we are asking them to do rather than just telling them.

Ask great questions and exhibit the right behaviours in front of customers so they can see the standard you expect.

6: Do you have well-understood and universally accepted rules of engagement?

Apart from the sales budgets they are all meant to achieve, have you also had a conversation about the standards of excellence and the accountability expectations, and have they fully committed to the achievement of these?

7: Do you have a clear message to market that all team members can recite and explain to prospects and clients?

A message to market that spells out your strategic uniqueness is a not-negotiable in today's competitive marketplace.

To be able to talk about our unique position in the market, our brand, our company background, and the range of products and services with confidence in a prepared but conversational way.

8: How high is the level of trust currently with your team?

How high of a priority is it for you to grow the trust of your team with your leadership?

9: How well is your sales team doing at gaining trust from your customers?

Have you sat down and worked with your salespeople to

create a plan of attack with each account and looking at behaviours that are trustworthy?

10: Are you constantly wearing the backpack and not delegating and empowering others?

You can't do it all. Your job is to work through your sales team. Too often, sales leaders jump in and rescue the sales team with dragging in opportunities rather than coaching the sales team to be more resourceful.

11: Are you running a sales meeting that is a victory march or are people dragging their feet when they leave the room?

Are they punching the air with excitement every time they leave the sales meeting? Having a strict start and finish time, a well-thought out agenda, and a motivational atmosphere is a must.

12: Do you know what the goals and motivators are of your sales team members individually?

Like a great AFL coach, we need to be in touch with every goal of every sales team member and what motivates them. No one salesperson is the same.

13: Do you know what your sales team activity and conversion rates are for all incoming leads?

Do you know your critical numbers? Reverse engineer the

results required for each team member and then work out what that means for contacts made and the conversion expected.

14: Can your sales team protect margin by building a business case and/or price justification model?

We need our sales team to be able to protect price and not give away all the profit in the deal.

Have you developed a price justification model with the team to justify the premium you charge over lost cost competitors?

15: Does your team own their numbers and understand the gap between current and expected performance?

We need to instil in our salespeople the desire to run their business inside the business by owning their individual budgets.

16: Are you attracting great new talent in recruiting from the market by living and breathing an employer-of-choice mindset and positioning?

No longer are all salespeople lucky to just have a job. We must attract new talent, then create a comprehensive induction program to make your business as an employer of choice.

17: Does your team go higher, wider, and deeper by mining all opportunities in the current client base?

There is a ton of gold in every database and CRM system. Are your salespeople conducting professional account planning and account reviews to uncover any new opportunities?

So, how did you do with the 17 questions? Got it all mastered? Then you don't need me anymore.

Still got work to do? Come join me and let's draw back the curtains on the exciting journey of a sales leader.

CHAPTER 3

A Changing Market – Understanding the Challenges Your Sales Team are Facing

It's a changing world and understanding the new sales environment is critical to your role in being able to maximise the performance of your team.

It also lets you work out where you will need to be strategic and direct the team, identifying the skill gaps and processes that need to be developed.

Here are the **10 challenges** I see in all teams with winning business and increasing competitive advantage at the moment with the new buying landscape:

1. Information is no longer power.

"Infobesity" is the word currently used to describe the glut of information available at everybody's fingertips.

Old-style salespeople get caught in a time warp and press on with "features and benefits selling" that worked in the distant past. Buyers want relationships and not just information; they want salespeople they can trust.

2. Your buyer is busier than ever before.

People trust professionals. Demonstrate your professionalism by not wasting the buyer's time and by responding quickly to inquiries. Your buyer's time is the most valuable asset they've got. They don't need to meet you unless there's something to discuss. In a challenging market, buyers might also be asked to stretch to cover more bases; chatting with vendors is not always the first priority.

3. There are only tiny differences between most competing products.

Product differences are decreasing between competing brands. Examples: generic peanuts versus branded peanuts, this fridge versus that fridge, this ream of A4 paper versus that ream.

The difference between anything from soap to same-class vehicles is very little. Not only that, an explanation of the difference can be boring if it's technical only by nature.

4. Your buyer is commoditising your team.

Customers don't buy on price, even though sometimes it sure feels that way (I can hear you say!).

Even though there are only tiny differences between competing products, there can be wide price differences.

Some people say there are only two places to be in the market: the premium end or the bottom end. They don't want to be lost in the murky middle. That's a terrible place to be; it's "me too" and "no apparent differentiation."

Requests for Proposals (RFPs) are an example of this where you are asked to fill in a spreadsheet and submit your best price.

Government departments and local government are great examples of this; if you are the incumbent, you are at a massive advantage as you play a role in writing the specifications that just happen to be your product.

5. Your buyer is trying to diminish the sales process.

Buyers are saying, "I don't want to talk to a salesperson unless I have to. I'll send out a spreadsheet with my needs and they can submit their best price. "Get them to email back their quote. I haven't got the time to speak with the sales guy!" That's a whole different selling game and it's happening more and more.

What game do you want to play? Is it a non-negotiable that

you get face-to-face with the potential buyer?

Do you have a minimum return on your time and energy as a service provider and know of other markets that value what you do that may provide a premium.

6. The market is more connected than ever.

Not everybody wants to get into Instagram or Facebook, but social media has a professional function and it's here to stay. Ignore at your own peril. Its function is about connecting to build business.

Connecting is a way to start the conversation, no argument there. But here's the trap a lot of salespeople have fallen into: they believe that sitting at a desk and Facebooking is selling.

Salespeople who have been around for a while know that there are always bright and shiny objects at any time in your selling life.

As the sales leader, are you being specific with your expectations as to how you want them spending their time?

7. The days of "turn up, suck up" customer visits are fast disappearing.

Back in the old days of selling, salespeople had a regular call cycle where they simply turned up with brochures and samples and chatted while bringing the brochures out one by one.

Regular call cycles today need to be questioned.

The question is, do you think your sales team is adding value?

If the buyer doesn't think they are, they will be despatched quickly and asked to come back less frequently with something to discuss. The sales team needs to be drilled and rehearsed in freshening up their meetings and making sure there is always a compelling reason to visit.

I remember coaching a team many years ago who were selling into retail outlets a range of products on 30 and 60 day cycles (depending on the size of the client).

One thing that became critically important was pre-planning together our visits up to three months ahead with slow release of new products and marketing promotions for the purpose of keeping things fresh.

8. Acquiring new customers is an increasingly costly process.

They say it used to cost six times as much to create a new customer as hanging onto an old one. I'm sure that getting a new client now is more like 20 times the cost of retaining an existing one. The high cost of acquiring new customers means you've got to (1) hang onto them with a big bear hug and (2) go higher, wider, and deeper than ever before looking for organic growth opportunities.

Learning how we leapfrog business from one to the next by

going higher, wider, and deeper rather than spending a fortune on advertising is key. The low-cost, easy way of getting new clients is through referrals and introductions.

9. Rote learned sales techniques are easily detected.

Throw out all the formatted and manipulative sales techniques. Customers spot them a mile away.

They read about them in magazines, see them exposed on news programs, and get internet warnings.

I remember many years ago I asked a couple of bookkeepers to pitch for my business as I was getting sick and tired of doing my own accounts, and let's face it, it doesn't make any sense at all for me to do it.

One of the bookkeepers must have attended an introductory sales course somewhere and rote learned an approach right down to the exact language the trainer gave them.

They asked, "So tell me, what keeps you awake at night?"

This was just too canned, it was a question I had heard over and over again out in the market. I couldn't help myself and replied, "Nothing really, I sleep pretty well." Find an approach that is yours, adapt the language and the questioning in the sales process, but don't just lift it out of a manual.

10. Your buyer doesn't want to be HARD SOLD to.

Connect with me, nurture me, but don't try to hard sell me right from the start! This is the mantra of the buyer today—they can smell an assertive hard sell from a mile away.

Buyers want to feel valued; they want to feel that you are acting with integrity and a desire to help.

A hard sell message out of context sticks out like a sore thumb; it's kind of uncomfortable, isn't it? It needs to be a natural progression of the selling conversation for it to be meaningful and successful.

I am not saying we shouldn't ask for the business; of course not, just time your run well.

Your sales team needs to be "re-tooled" to accommodate these new pressures from the discerning buyer. How well do you understand these current-day pressures and how often do you work with them to come up with a sales plan for achievement?

CHAPTER 4

Putting on Your Own Oxygen Mask First!

In so many sales teams I have worked with, the sales manager is the highest paid sales role in the business.

Whilst there is no logic to this as they are two very different jobs; it just is. With this in mind, we need to consider the huge cost on the business if you don't take care of yourself first.

The company will run the risk of not functioning with the same sales precision and this can be very expensive.

A Coach for the Coach

All great leaders should have coaches working with them. It just makes sense to have a third-party opinion and a range of perspectives. Same with the sales leader. You don't have all the answers and need, from time to time, clarity from a sounding board. Perhaps a mentor relationship from a person who has good business experience, perhaps running their own business?

Perhaps you need more than one specialist in different areas who can craft a piece of your sales leader's toolbox for you.

I think it's hard to speak of the virtues of the external coach unless you have experienced the benefits of the coaching relationship yourself. Since I can remember, I have enlisted the help of mentors and coaches in my career. At first it was typically semi-retired previous business owners who helped me with the fundamentals of running my own business, from finance to marketing to HR.

Now, as a consultant, speaker, coach, and writer, I have enlisted overseas speaking coaches, consultant coaches, and training coaches to help me to get better and to be that person who will not listen to excuses when they hear them.

I know they will have my interests at heart and know clearly what it will take for me to progress, to be better this month than last month.

I have found that having deadlines set, homework assigned, and to be shown why it's important has always kept me focused on delivering the best outcomes to my clients.

So, if you don't have a coach, interview one. See if you feel there is a values alignment and look for a proven track record. It will be worth the investment.

Get Out of the Pressure Cooker

The pressures of sales leadership are real. Every month there is a determination as to whether the sales department is "doing their job." I think because there are certain metrics that are clear, such as sales volume, gross margins, units sold, etc., it is easy to notice whether the department is on target.

Sure, other departments in the business have metrics as well, it's just that the sales department is under scrutiny more often. Given that your role is a pressured role, your ability to look after your health is paramount.

Find a mental outlet, whether that be feeding the mind with ideas and creative thinking or no thinking at all. Also, create a physical outlet where you can get away from it all.

Learn meditation, go to the gym, try a new hobby—just find a release so you can maintain perspective in your role.

Creating a Weekly Schedule That Works

Creating your own schedule for a productive week is paramount to being a great sales leader. The truth is that most sales managers are immersed with their team, and whatever time they have left over then becomes their own.

This is not thinking strategically. To be always available to the team, to have the open door policy, just doesn't work. You need to create boundaries, and you need to have some really productive time when you are the freshest for you.

Let the team know there are certain times in the week when you are not available. Most of the time the sales team will be able to deal with it. Try it. It's amazing how resourceful they can be.

So what are the big rocks that need to go into your week as you are organising your week?

You need time to have the sales meeting, time to do planning for the week, month, and quarter, to plan stock purchases, to look at current promotions to see what is working, to plan future promotions, and schedule in the time for the one-to-one coaching sessions. You need time to think.

This is the stuff you are actually paid to do.

Running the Team from Coffee Shops

When I ran my team, I would make it a practice to be out of the office and working from home for half a day each week.

For me, a carefully chosen coffee shop that never really got busy was ideal; have a few of them up your sleeve. I used to always make a pact with myself that I would treat myself with bacon and eggs and a nice coffee in return for a 7.30 a.m. start.

In, say, three hours, I would almost get more done than

during the remainder of the week for strategic time. You see, it was totally uninterrupted work. For some whom I have mentored, working from home was an option. If working from home isn't an option, then consider having a few alternative places you can go to and work. When I suggest this to coaching clients, you can see them flinch, as if there was no way this could be achieved. However, when they realized that during the time that were not in the office the place didn't burn down, they fully embraced the concept.

You Need to Shape Your Team

As a sales leader (especially if you have inherited a team from the previous sales manager), one of the most important things you need to do is to shape the team with the calibre of talent you are looking for.

That means if someone is not going to make it, then it's up to you to be decisive and act fairly quickly.

The old expression "hire slow and fire fast" is true, as it will only cause you stress trying to help those who can't be helped.

Most sales managers spend more than 80 percent of their time on the 20 percent of salespeople on their team who are high maintenance and unable to achieve their sales targets.

Be careful, the payoff comes from working with the best salespeople and making them better.

Leading by Example, There is No Other Way

Don't expect your sales team to do all the tough stuff while you manage from the desk.

Don't escape the hard conversations with clients, when the sales team needs you to troubleshoot be available.

A great sales leader needs to constantly evolve and add value to the sales team. This means troubleshooting and jumping in when a more strategic mind is required.

Your team will admire the effort; they will get inspiration from the fact that you "have their back."

If you want the team to canvass regularly, get amongst them and make some calls or visit industrial estates with them to keep the edge.

I go out on sales calls with salespeople all the time when I am coaching a team, it's amazing how often I hear from salespeople that their manager never goes out with them.

Fragile Confidence

Sales leadership is not about being bulletproof.

It's natural to question yourself, to be uncertain, to be anxious about presenting to the team, to craft a large new business pitch with a new account in tandem with some of the team or perhaps even organizing the yearly national sales conference.

I remember speaking at the national sales conference of a client where the national sales manager was brand new to the role. He was nervous about the conference not working out well for the team.

Once I explained to him that this was quite natural and that these fears were about something that hadn't happened yet, he settled down and we got on with planning the theme and the sessions for the conference. The fear was false evidence appearing real (not mine by the way), there was no evidence attached to the reality. Once he realised the sales team were looking forward to getting together and sharing ideas and war stories, he then remained calm.

It was a roaring success, by the way.

Self-doubt and the subsequent procrastination in sales leadership can be challenging in getting things done with the team. It also sends a poor leadership message to the team, salespeople want their leader to be decisive.

The challenge with sales leaders' self-confidence levels is that they tend to rise and fall with short-term success and perceived failure based on weekly and monthly sales results.

The goal we are trying to achieve as a sales leader is to maintain some type of consistency in our self-confidence and not make it mirror the month's sales results.

We need to take a longer term view, to stay the course with

the plan and to communicate with the stakeholders above of our progress.

Ask yourself:

Do you find yourself flip-flopping on decisions based on others' feedback?

Do your moods shift each month according to the sales actual versus target without a long-term focus?

Do you stubbornly stay the course when it becomes obvious that there needs to be changes made in terms of personnel or strategy?

Do you allow yourself to be pushed around by strong senior sales professionals on your team?

Do you avoid confrontation at all costs with other departments in the business when you know that one of the sales team has dropped the ball on expectations?

These are common things I see. By the way, it's not nearly as bad as we let our mind conjure it up to be.

The moral of the story—go to work on yourself first. Don't band aid your own future but spend some time on creating a new direction with expectations and not negotiables for you.

PART A
Transformational Thinking

Transforming the Sales Team

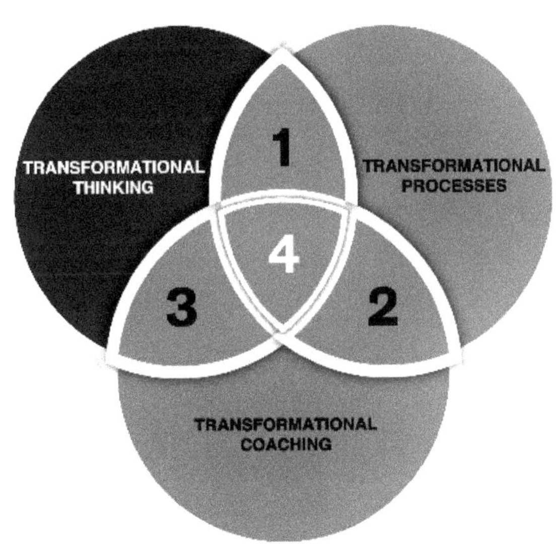

Transforming the Sales Team Starts with the Way *You* Think...

As a sales manager, it's all about the daily grind and being so busy that you can't think.

As a sales leader, it's about working smarter and creating new paradigms that allow us to be strategists.

Our thinking needs to shift: how we see our role, how we see the sales professionals' roles, how we plan for the next 12 months and beyond, how we see the type of environment we want to create.

I always think that good strategic thinking requires us to reverse engineer, to ask ourselves what that future looks like, and then to transform our thinking to be open to new ways and new tactics to achieve it.

If you could start again with your team in your role, what would go on the blank page as being the non-negotiables to your thinking?

CHAPTER 5

The Mindset Shift: Distinctions of Great Sales Leaders

Transforming our thinking starts with the ability to think about our role differently.

Perhaps we need to reframe our responsibility and look at things from a different angle.

A sales leader lives by a number of distinctions to be successful in their role as a leader of their team:

1. The Great Privilege of Sales Leadership

You determine the direction, create the plan, and execute the plan with the team. It's an enormous privilege to lead the team.

Think of your growth and development, the journey you

have been on since you started in sales. Who was an early mentor to you in sales? Who gave you some of the valuable lessons of sales?

Who taught you the way to hold yourself on a sales call, the ability to manage your time effectively, the person who shared great language and questions to ask?

We know that sales leadership is not a 9 to 5 job. It requires you to think of each person on the team and how you can get the most out of them, it never stops.

Never lose sight of the fact that you are playing with people's lives; this is an enormous responsibility. We will see the best of them, when they are punching the air, and we will see them when they are frustrated and perhaps doubting their ability.

You are also a role model, someone they look to for guidance and inspiration. Never underestimate the obligation and responsibility that comes with the position.

2. Your Ultimate Responsibility is Sales Growth

Sounds like a strange thing to say, I know.

However, I wish I could have a dollar for every time that I coached a sales manager and could see that their mind was filled with everything but actually achieving the growth in the business. Administrivia, coordinating orders, chasing payment, etc., you get the idea.

As a sales leader, you lead the sales growth of the business to increase market share and expand the sales base.

Use your "important and not urgent" time to design the vision of the future, to create the sales game plan, and to get engagement for the plan.

Then your job is to make the understanding of that plan easy—to provide a template for how that grand plan can be achieved. The bottom line is this: If the business is not growing, you are not doing your job.

3. Proactive and Not Reactive

Great sales leaders proactively coach and mentor; they jump on the front foot when they can sense that something isn't right. They have their eyes and ears close to the ground, to sense when something doesn't feel right in terms of achieving the monthly and quarterly targets. They have a sixth sense for when something just doesn't feel right—your experience will alert you to it.

You don't get surprises at the end of the month when salespeople report in on their pipelines. You already know when someone is struggling; you have met with them and spent time looking at activity.

You know the impact of losing a major account, and you

double down on creating new opportunities throughout the team to fill the gap.

You create team responsibility and inspire action.

4. Constantly Sharpening the Saw of the Team

Sales leaders understand that they don't have all the answers and that sometimes they need to be upskilling by learning about the skills of being a sales leader.

They challenge themselves and they constantly challenge the sales professionals to get better, to find a better process, to improve their language and role play the delivery.

The need for ongoing training is not a nice to have, it's a "must have."

Sales managers make the incorrect assumption that a salesperson with years of experience will not have to be trained on introductory concepts.

This is the hoodwinking that the sales leader won't buy into. They know that even if they were trained years ago, things change. Training and coaching is all about skills, but it's also about the right mindset and the positive shot of mojo the team requires to be at their best.

A personal development plan for your sales team is critical to the ability to convert more business rather than just doing more and more calls for lower results.

5. Walking Your Talk

If you want your team to follow your leadership, then take pride in following through on your talk.

If the direction is to go to industrial estates and do introduction calls every Tuesday morning, then make sure you are there with them at least most of the time.

You don't always have to be the best at it, just your positive presence and enthusiasm will work wonders for the team morale.

If you need to have the team coordinate and do the meet-and-greet at an exhibition stand at a yearly conference expo for days, then turn up and do a cameo each day to meet the clients who visit and those who are looking for more information as prospects. Sales leadership is not about one set of rules for the team and one set of rules for you. It's about you holding yourself to account to the team when you get together and following through on your commitments.

6. Gut Instinct with Structured Thinking

Street smarts and gut instinct are important traits of the trusted sales leader. Equally is the ability to plan ahead with a structured and planned approach to sales team excellence.

Taking the guesswork out of sales leadership by building sales team processes with expected outcomes built on experience and results is key for the modern leader.

Creating systems that work, controlling the company data, and not relying on salespeople's scraps of notes and diary scribbles is now the minimum.

7. Always Benchmarking Outside the Industry

The sales leader who looks for a contrarian way to approach their industry with a new offering, a new method, or a new process creates a competitive advantage. This requires you to be well read, to attend conferences, to attend training programs, and to be creative in your thinking process. To be a game changer in your industry requires different thinking, thinking that many of your competitors haven't yet thought of.

The sales leader understands their role is to maximise the results of their individual team members, to work through their team to deliver the collective sales goal, and to do it in a way that it doesn't make them the bottleneck in the business.

Sales Leadership Transformer: Embrace your role. Understand what an honour it is to lead the team. Think about your commitment to your craft and getting better each day.

CHAPTER 6

The New Sales Leader - Proactively Seeing Trends Before They Happen!

Sales leadership is all about being proactive and aware in advance of any headwinds or deviations which might occur in achieving the sales results for the business.

Looking ahead to the future, there are several trends that have become key forces in sales team leadership. The future of selling always requires us to re-tool our mindset, re-tool our team's skills, and re-tool the way that we produce results.

There are **eight shifts** that I see that are on the radar for sales leaders right now in how to structure the sales team, create strategy, and produce sustainable advantage:

- Creating a more autonomous and mobile sales team
- Tapping into in a part-time sales force
- Taking advantage of the outsourcing phenomenon
- Getting clear on your competitive uniqueness to market
- Creating an "all in" trusted single enterprise where all departments are now part of the selling process
- Directing salespeople to choreograph their sales experiences and not just turning up for sales calls
- Embracing the virtual servicing of the "long tail" accounts by Zoom and other mediums so as to open up time to work on new business.
- Understanding collaboration is the way to build new business

Creating a More Autonomous and Mobile Sales Team

Great sales leaders understand it is not micro-managing that will get the results for them.

They need to trust that the sales team will be responsible for their numbers and the activities that produce results.

Sales teams have learned through the COVID-19 crisis to work alone, to be at home, and run their own schedule without being around the team.

This presents an enormous opportunity to review the company requirements for bricks-and-mortar, for company cars, and other resources that have been a part of the sales team for many years.

Now salespeople can use virtual office facilities, hot desking, and membership-based virtual offices to get the job done.

If one of the ways to produce sales team results is through increased productivity, then everything is on the table for consideration.

Some salespeople will work better by themselves and we have seen those who have thrived in that environment.

Ask yourself if your future results will come from completion of tasks and where people are sitting in the office or whether they will come from good strategy and managing performance standards?

Get the processes and the coaching (Section 3) right and you can create a team that can operate autonomously.

Think of the wasted time waiting in traffic to get to the office and then back home and deliver that extra time to your salespeople to achieve bigger results.

Sales Leadership Transformer: Consider a different way of working, the need for the office, the new focus on results and performance standards.

Tapping Into a Part-Time Salesforce

The 2020s and beyond will see an increase in available sales talent in the market based on a recovering economy.

If we take a strategic approach to achieving our sales budget each year, then perhaps there is an opportunity for us to engage in the part-time sales community to help us achieve our sales goal.

In my past life, we had a sales team in the seasonal diary and organiser business I previously owned before selling it in 2008. They were full-time sales employees and I think I convinced myself that it was the only way.

If I had my business now, I would be inclined to tap into the array of talent out there and create a model where a part-time approach could have worked more effectively after a thorough induction program.

Think of what you need to get the job done. It may be commonplace for professional salespeople to work at the same time for multiple organisations if their selling skills are easily transferable to that environment.

Sales Leadership Transformer: Throw out the old paradigms of how salespeople work. Create your own new rules by tapping into the wealth of knowledge and high calibre skills being underutilised.

Taking Advantage of the Outsourcing Phenomenon

Never have there been so many options for getting tasks completed overseas for our business.

Companies are now regularly using Upwork, Fiver, Guru, etc. to get brochures designed, to get websites completed, to work on sales collateral, and to create LinkedIn connections and social media posts.

Think of what is now a core activity in the business and what can be outsourced outside the team. There are no rules, it's whatever works for the business.

The jobs of creating a client, doing the face-to-face new business call and the follow-up, and putting together the sales proposal are all core activities at the front end. But… think about how you update your website, how you send out the email campaigns through your CRM system, prepare client newsletters, LinkedIn posts, etc. They can all be done offshore.

Certain jobs can be done productively no matter where people are sitting. The outsourcing phenomenon taps into a massive number of talented people around the world who can complete that task based on a fixed-project amount.

Think of a world with less permanent sales talent in the team and those admin functions that go with it. A world where salespeople are paid at a premium to do what they are employed to do: to sell.

The new way of leading a sales team is to consider what needs to be done and then to go about the market to buy those services in the most cost-effective and results-driven way.

Try posting a project or two and test the results. You will be surprised by how much you will save but also how succinct and outcome-focused you will be.

Sales Leadership Transformer: Posting a project means you can use your time effectively in the office and do what you are paid to do. No managing of support people all the time, just focus on the pointy end.

The Need to Get Clear on Your Competitive Uniqueness to Market

Business is as competitive as ever; acquiring new customers will take a very succinct approach to making our competitive advantage clear. The days of having "me too" language during the sales presentation will render you irrelevant. Our objective is to stand out right from the word go.

When I work with the client, developing a message to market is one of the first things we do together. It galvanizes the team, and it makes sure we know where true north is and how we fit in the market.

The secret is to create compelling reasons and language as

to why a new prospect should work with you. The benefits are enormous. When we know where we can outrun our competition, it gives the team a lift in mojo and reserve power in dealing with any objections in the sales process.

I have dedicated all of Chapter 15 to a process of formulation of your message to market. Challenge your team to get involved and to buy into the process.

> ***Sales Leadership Transformer: Don't caught up in the murky "me-too" middle. Stand out and cut through the noisy market with a statement that positions you in a category of one.***

Creating an "All In" Trusted Single Enterprise

Silo thinking is old thinking. Selling is everyone's business for us to be successful as the sales leader. The business we are in today is the true Trusted Single Enterprise: one business with one philosophy going to market.

When we understand that the business becomes more attractive to the client when there is consistency of experience and culture, we can wrap our arms around every new prospect, develop the relationship, and never let go.

The high cost of acquisition of a client means that retention is everything, but then so are referrals, and this is the by-product.

The benefits to the organisation are endless if they can get it right: increased loyalty factor of clients, increased overall sales due to cross-selling, up-selling opportunities, being the employer of choice due to a more harmonious work environment, and a consistency of messaging throughout the business and externally to the market. So, as the sales leader, how are you harnessing this culture and getting enthusiastic cooperation from the service, accounts, admin, marketing, or other departments?

Sales Leadership Transformer: Get other departments involved in your sales training, your sales meetings, and attend their meetings. Be the attractive enterprise that is magnetic.

Choreographed Customer Experiences and Not Just Making Sales Calls

The onus is on us to lift the bar with the team to make sure the customer experience is more than a habitual sales call on a regular cycle. The challenge of getting face-to-face appointments will continue in this decade and beyond when compared to how selling has been done in the past as buyers have got used to being able to work virtually.

We need to show the sales team how to craft their presentation, to maximize the engagement level, and to choreograph and rehearse what is a memorable experience.

Role playing the questions we ask, how to segue into the main business, how to create and deliver a message of uniqueness, to provide a compelling argument, and to ask for the business or create next steps is a key part to our coaching role.

Managing the activity KPIs is only one part of the mix. How do we quality assure what is being presented? Our sales management edict in the past was to simply manage the contacts and not the results and maximize the impact they have.

Sales Leadership Transformer: What's your method for constant process improvement so you are getting a higher level of conversion and not just a bigger pipeline?

Embracing the Virtual Servicing of the Long Tail of Accounts

Zoom and other online seminar and meeting software will continue to be an efficient and effective way to make the account servicing calls to our clients. Instead of having to call on clients physically for "long tail" type sales where we are reconfirming a smaller order, we can continue to show the sales team how to have these conversations online.

I have a financial planning client, and their whole team has been using Zoom for those client coaching calls for some time and will continue to make sure it's a part of the way they do business.

When you are discussing numbers, investments, and performance of the portfolio, is there always a compelling reason for the financial planners to have to meet face to face when it's part of the quarterly coaching?

Travel distances and traffic now means that every sales experience face to face is golden time. Save it for the account development work or where there is organic sales growth opportunities, referral conversations, and the new business introduction calls.

Sales Leadership Transformer: Zoom has changed the way we think of business. We now can be efficient and effective by scheduling time virtually and still making it an experience.

Understanding Collaboration is the Way to Build New Business

Acquisition of new clients is expensive work if we are not strategic and tactical about our process.

One of the best ways for us to "create rain," or new clients and business development, is through referrals and introductions.

Every sales team I address tells me that they can get a good deal better at getting referrals, and the language associated with it, a lot better. We need to instruct and show our sales team how to collaborate in the market to create more.

The key skills we need to model for them are the ability to:

- Gain referrals
- Develop referrals into trusted introductions
- Ask for recommendations and testimonials
- Network in their industry and business groups
- Build and be a part of communities

All these activities cost nothing in business!

When you consider the cost of other prospecting such as telemarketing services, sponsorship, outbound mailing and electronic mail exhibitions, and expos and other advertising, this is the key mindset we need our sales team to have.

It is no longer a "nice to have" skill—these are must haves of the modern sales team, and we need to put the resources in place to develop this part of the business.

Sales Leadership Transformer: Show the sales team how to get better at asking the referral and introduction questions. Track and measure their success and see the opportunities appear.

CHAPTER 7

Everyone is in the Business of Sales

Daniel Pink put it well in *To Sell is Human* when he said:

"We're all in sales now. We're persuading, convincing, and influencing others to give up something they've got in exchange for what we've got."

The business of tomorrow will recognize the importance of everyone being on the sales team. As much as sales have the title, every contact the customer has with the company and its personnel will create an impression as to whether or not they want to continue to engage the company.

I call it a true Trusted Single Enterprise.

So how would you know if you were to come across a Trusted Single Enterprise?

The best example I can give is Apple and the passion they have for what they do. They were a true game changer in their space with the Apple shops around the world. Do you own an Apple product? Chances are that you do. Go into an Apple retail shop and see complete engagement in the product at the coal face, training of the product ongoing for their customers, and a genius bar to make sure the product is being well supported.

I think it's easy to overlook how they changed the environment in which they compete. Just think for a moment about what it looked like before they entered at retail level.

If you wanted a service technician to come and service or repair, you had to wait for them to show, personal hygiene wasn't a high priority, and just when they would get into your problem, they would be called away to the next job.

Every business puts across a message of "caring for the customer" and "making the customer No. 1," but informed customers are cynical about that propaganda. Nowadays, a business has to earn their customers' trust. And to do so, every person in the business has a role to play. Customers come in contact with many people inside your business (or the enterprise you work for). In every customer point of contact, every team member has to live up to your sales promises, lest they turn you into a liar without you even knowing!

Consider the following:

1: Are there rules of engagement within the company in how all departments deal with customers?

2: Do you have a message to market in terms of the way you talk about the business for all staff to follow when talking with every customer?

3: If the sales responsibility is isolated to a particular department, will the customer receive the same level of care from the rest of the company as promised by the person doing the selling?

It doesn't matter whether the staffer is at the front desk, in the back room, or on the selling room floor, everyone is in the business of selling.

So how are you going to tell your accounts department that they are in the business of selling? And what's in it for them?

There are more selling opportunities than people think. In the case of parts and service department in a car dealership, it's not unusual that there'll be an opportunity if a vehicle with 150,000 km on the clock is being serviced, the mechanic sees it's starting to fall apart and gets a spotter's fee if he or she can get the salesperson to create a sale.

There's an old saying in the automotive industry that the sales department makes the first sale and the service department makes the second, third, and fourth.

Service people are trusted advisors in being able to develop that relationship. Encourage them to have that communication and conversation with the buyers.

Darren Sprigg from award winning South West ISUZU in Picton, WA, is a great client of mine and captures the strength of the Single Enterprise:

> "Surely the responsibility of leadership is to get the absolute best out of their leadership and the individuals within it. It is the organisation that sets a culture, and it is the leadership that makes sure the organisation instils, reinforces, improves the culture. Leadership needs to be flipped on its head. The Single Enterprise is the greatest achievement of all. It's not easy but it's rewarding."

There is a common goal.

We are all part of an enterprise that is responsible for transferring trust to the customer.

We all have that job to do and a role to play in terms of being able to hold the company in a unique good light.

Find ways to allow opportunities to emerge.

In agricultural sales, it is the technician who arrives on the farm and is greeted with scones and cups of tea while the salesperson turning up in the new 4WD is left waiting.

Trust is earned and is a reflection of the promise made for the farmer: "when your light is on, our light is on."

The qualities of the **Trusted Single Enterprise** are:

- They have a common goal and purpose
- They work as one team to market
- They have a commitment to personal and business excellence
- They are resilient and can lift under pressure
- They understand the value of the long-term partnership with client
- They are all brand ambassadors of the business in the market and wear the logo with pride
- They have agreed rules of engagement

Creating a sales culture throughout the organisation is critical to gain a true competitive advantage and to make it hard to infiltrate your customer base for a new or low-priced alternative. One way of looking like an integrated enterprise is to think of the flow of events that happens in the mind of the buyer.

Firstly, the Marketing Promise...

The marketing department is charged with the responsibility of having enough qualified buyers put their hand up to want to know more. However, if the brand positioning is not right and the marketing collateral provides a confusing message, it leads to more unqualified leads that do not wish to pay the price. Our job is to feed back to marketing the response from the coal face, what the customer is actually telling us.

This is an overlooked critical aspect of business.

Then, the Sales Experience...

On first impression, the sales department must be responsive and ready to discuss further the possible opportunity.

The conflict that needs to be managed is when the marketing department believes it is providing a great number of qualified leads and there is frustration with a lower than acceptable conversion rate.

So how are you instructing the sales team to give feedback to marketing, but also to let marketing know when they have converted an opportunity?

When I had my business, I always reminded the salespeople to go and let the telemarketers know that they had success with a lead generated.

The telemarketers were desk bound, never saw the customer, and only had the phone call to rely on. They loved it when the sales team went out of the way to let them know what a critical role they were playing in the company.

Finally, the Service Delivery...

Now it is over to service to deliver on the order taken by sales in terms of fulfilment of the expectation. Service believe that sales are making promises they can't keep and therefore are saying anything to the customer to get the order.

Your role is to manage the backend relationship, to make sure the sales team isn't checking every five minutes on their order because that's the order they make the commission on!

Everyone plays their role and the machine breaks down if there isn't a clever flow between these critical contact periods.

Spend a moment to map it out and look for where cracks appear in the client experience and you will be multiple steps ahead of your competitors.

Five "Culture Shifts" for a Trusted Single Enterprise

I am often asked "so how do we get started on this road together and increase the level of communication between the departments?"

1. ***Marketing needs to be more involved in the coal face of the selling machine.*** Go out on calls and listening to the customer to see what the expectation is, then they can reverse engineer all marketing collateral.
2. ***Sales must understand that a lead is an opportunity and not a chance to whinge*** about the quality of the

lead. The customer is ringing in and asking about what your offer is; what a great opportunity to up-sell from the offer and get a conversation started.

3. ***Service and sales need to do more joint calls together*** to understand the customer, to build a better relationship internally, and then the handover and the servicing of that account will be seamless. This will also ensure we are on top of the next client opportunity to re-purchase the product or service.
4. ***Sales and service must attend each other's meetings.*** Get involved with a representative of each department contributing to the conversation at the other's meeting.
5. ***More "whole of business" meetings.*** Everyone needs to come together to hear the big picture and know the achievements of each department and the company overall.

Sales Leadership Transformer: The Trusted Single Enterprise is a powerful organisation. Make the start and increase the level of communication so you can begin the journey.

CHAPTER 8

How Do You See Your Sales Team? Order Takers or Trusted Advisors?

When coaching and training salespeople, I am always looking for the keys that a great salesperson must be good at to be even better.

Over the years, it has become clear to me that when we look for salespeople in our organisation, we can bring it all down to five key areas.

My Trusted Advisor Method in selling identifies these **five key attributes:**

- A Strategic Thinker
- A Value Creator
- A Dealmaker
- A Rainmaker
- A Trust Maker

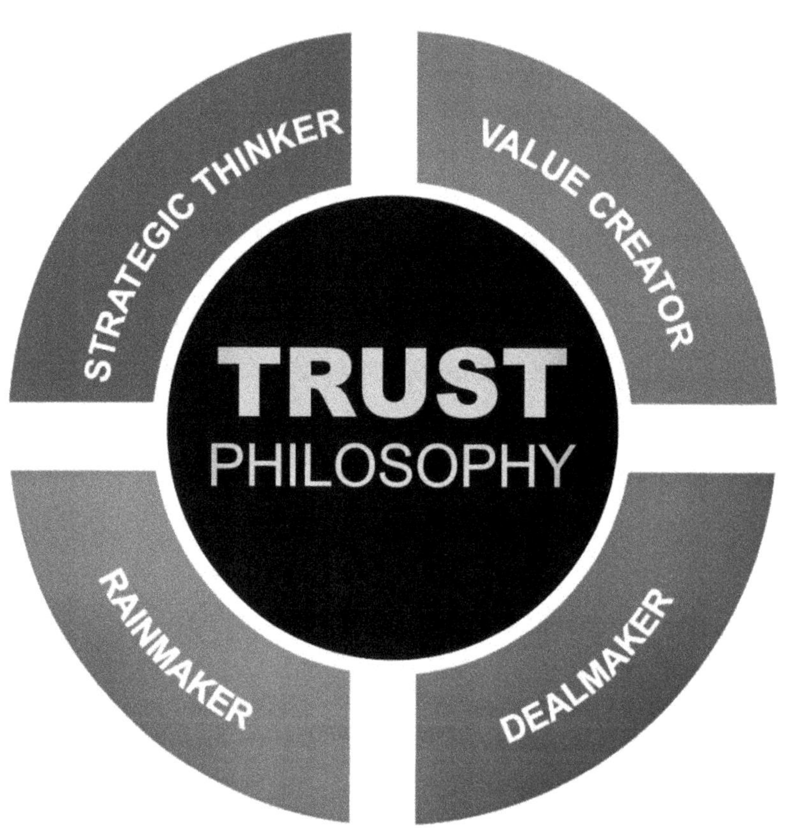
STRATEGIC THINKER
VALUE CREATOR
TRUST
PHILOSOPHY
RAINMAKER
DEALMAKER

The Strategic Thinker

Thinking like a "business inside the business" is fundamental to salesperson success as a strategic thinker. Trusted advisors think of themselves as a product in the market for which the company pays them for their smarts.

Salespeople need to create a master plan that takes into account their key performance markers, their marketing activities, their skill development plan, and their plan for each current account they have in their portfolio.

A strategic thinker understands the critical sales numbers, and the determinants of how they will achieve their budget will be fundamental.

Tracking and measuring your numbers against these key criteria is a sought after skill.

They understand the 80/20 rule where you manage your time accordingly and understand that you need to put your trust into other departments of the business to implement the sales orders as you confirm them.

Things to look for with the strategic thinker attribute:

1. Does the salesperson know how to develop their one-page success plan?
2. Do they know how to reverse engineer their numbers to meet and exceed their sales budget?

3. Do they know the critical nature of speed as a competitive advantage?
4. Do they understand the four core drivers of all customers?
5. Do they know how to build an answer to the #1 question in sales: "Why, out of all the vendors available to me, should I buy from your company?"
6. Does each salesperson have a one-line Trusted advisor value proposition?

The Value Creator

The value creator thinks differently from the salesperson who discounts at every turn. They understand margin and holding it in the sale, they are subject matter experts and will always be looking for ways to cover the product knowledge gap.

The buyer wants someone who can tell them like it is, no BS, just the facts. They also want someone who they know might be a little more premium but they deliver well and beyond what is expected.

By being able to make respectful "apples versus oranges" comparisons with competing products and solutions, the value creator holds their ground and is a true friend to the confused buyer. Buyers will continue to ask us to justify our price.

We therefore need to arm ourselves with some tactical ways

of making our value argument.

Trusted advisors don't hide from "putting the elephant in the room" if they know that there is a price discrepancy between their solution and a competing one, and they will meet any objection head on. There will always be a lower cost producer in every market. It's a race to the bottom if you get sucked into that way of thinking. Being a value creator requires you to sell the expertise, time, and the care to put into the sale, which big business does **not.**

The word "cheap" is a good word to use when stigmatising low cost competitors. Deride the word "cheap" in your negotiations.

When helping a client who has a premium product, I coach them on letting their buyers know that in any market, there is always a low-cost cheap competitor and I will deliberately accentuate the word "cheap." When weighed against quality, "cheap" always sounds tacky.

Trusted advisors get paid on making more gross margin rather than just sales turnover dollars, so even if we make the sale, is the sales worth having in the first place?

Things to look for with the value creator attribute:

1. Does the team know how to deal with the price-driven buyer?

2. Can they develop a business case to show lowest total cost solution?
3. Can they create questions that take the focus off price and on to building a "right fit solution"?
4. Do they understand the phrases, questions, and words that disrupt the price-driven buyer?
5. Can they listen and repeat back effectively the points raised during a client meeting?

The Dealmaker

The essence of deal making is understanding people, understanding what makes them tick, and the power of language. Being a dealmaker means we need to start with the right mindset for success.

The dealmaker attribute has continued to evolve over time, with a "hard closer" mentality not being purely a quality for success. Buyers are smarter now and can sense a strong sales message when they are not ready to buy and will go underground if they feel that they are being forced into a decision. A dealmaker needs to strategise and think through the deal in front of them, they need to engage all stakeholders.

They need to work the conversation in their mind before going into any buyer negotiation, and then they need to be bold enough to ask for the business in a respectful way.

They also know that they will need a sales process that works but is flexible in approach so it doesn't sound like it's rote learned. The theatre of the sale, the benefits of great language, the questions that are asked, and the evidence to be provided to create a compelling business case.

Things to look for with the deal maker attribute:

1. Do they know how to close more business more often, for more money?
2. Do they have a step-by-step sales process?
3. Do they understand the great power of storytelling?
4. How are their questioning skills to engage your buyer?
5. Are they aware of words that sell and words that don't sell?
6. Do they know the sources of power in a negotiation?

The Rainmaker

The key fundamental of being the rainmaker is about having multiple streams of opportunities at any one time. They are able to continually attract referrals and introductions, be sticky in the market, and know what works for their overall results.

Rainmaking also takes patience.

You're not going to get a result straight away. If I go out in the street and start knocking on doors, I'm not going to get instant success. I'm going to have to go back and see them repeatedly before I clinch it. So rainmaking takes patience.

As a sales leader, you are looking for the ability to nurture the sale from the initial introduction through to the first order, to be able to keep up contact levels beyond the initial connection made, and to warm the prospect up by showing a genuine interest. Some people don't return calls. That's always been the case, but it's more so now. Many salespeople find this really hard to understand, especially sole trader business owners in service businesses when they are just starting out.

I think we as salespeople get what we deserve sometimes. We leave a message and then when the person rings back, we don't have a plan for the call but simply say, "I was just ringing to see how you were and to have a chat."

Things to look for with the Rainmaker attribute:

1. Can they create multiple streams of opportunities for their pipeline?
2. Can they create a mountain of referrals?
3. Can they go "higher, wider, and deeper" to increase business from current customers?
4. Do they know how to nurture the lead and go deeper with the prospect?
5. Can they track and measure the results of every lead, to know the status of the opportunity at any time?
6. Are they resourceful by self-generating opportunities and not relying on the company to give them all their leads?

The Trust Maker

The trusted advisor in selling is proud of their vocation and really believes they are part of a noble profession. They sell with pride and energy that makes them attractive in the market.

They respect their buyers' time and will confirm in advance, will be punctual, and will work within agreed time frames for the meetings. They know that when they say they will do something that they are on show and better meet the promise made.

Being consistent with the client interaction, providing clarity in the way they explain the solution and also the answers to client questions, and exhibiting competency provides a thought leader positioning in the mind of the buyer.

"All business is based on trust" is a saying you've probably often heard. It's critical in business-to-business selling. The trust maker builds a relationship on trust, customers will stay with them longer.

Trust is the reason to go further with a salesperson. Transparency leads to trust. A common purpose and a common background builds trust. These are all part of a connecting point.

So what are the skills that we need in our sales team when we set the standards for performance?

Things to look for with the trust maker attribute:

1. Do they know what creates trust today in the mind of the buyer?
2. How are they at creating likeability for longevity of relationship with your buyer?
3. Can they determine the buying style of your customer and blending with your selling style?
4. Do they make speed their first priority in maintaining the trust of your customer?
5. Do they honour their promises and not create unnecessary stress in the delivery chain to the customer?

Sales Leadership Transformer: How does your team match up with these 5 key attributes of the trusted advisor? Where do they need to improve and thrive?

CHAPTER 9
The Sales Culture You Want!

I remember speaking at a sales conference last year and the speaker before me was Paul Roos, the Sydney and Melbourne AFL ex-coach. We had a quick chat before his presentation and talked about culture in organisations.

He made an interesting comment and said that "even if you don't think you have a culture, you have a culture."

When I work with a new client sales team on selling skills, sales process, and structures, I always start with questioning and digging deep into the current and desired sales culture for the organisation.

You can feel the culture of the organisation within the first morning working there.

It's even more apparent when you are a consultant to a sales team and you attend their first sales meeting—you really get a sense of how things are going and how much the sales team are behind the message.

Your job as the sales leader is to be the leader of the sales culture you want. You help create the environment for the right inputs and then craft the feedback from the team to create a strong message and plan.

How a Great Sales Culture will create results

A well-defined and agreed-upon sales culture will produce long-term results as it:

- Provides an agreement between all stakeholders as to what we hold dear and true
- Makes clear the things we stand for and those things that are unacceptable
- Quantifies the key numbers we have set as a measurement of the progress towards our objective
- Puts your stamp on the team as the sales leader as to what your direction and strategy is
- Provides a deeper client connection and client experience in every contact with customers and also prospects
- Solidifies our purpose

Great sales cultures matter, they are the backbone of the team. They are the guiding force behind coming to work each day and give us purpose in our pursuits.

As the sales leader, we want a team that takes pride in their work and to feel like they are a part of something special, it makes for a cohesive unit and it makes good business sense with the high cost of recruitment.

What Culture Do You Really Want?

Getting the room temperature right for that culture conversation is where we start and then we build from there.

I was asked to come to Newcastle by the CEO of a financial planning company and to work with the team for one day early in my consulting business. It was to be a team building workshop where the team would bond and develop their plan together.

It was fascinating to me on arrival how you could sense the atmosphere. I got to the room early and started to make small talk with the participants while we were waiting for the MD to arrive. They were really quiet and I wondered how the day would go—were they engaged with the workshop purpose, were they interested in setting some goals as a team?

Chris came swashbuckling through the door and made sure everyone knew he was there. He was a dominant assertive

CEO who knew exactly how he wanted the day to go. He had a clear agenda. I soon realised the workshop was designed to send a message to the staff rather than asking for their opinions. He was looking to make a point as he thought the business was under-performing.

The day was all very positive except for Chris's constant interruptions that broke a train of thought for participants.

The culture of the organisation was an autocratic culture, the reason why people didn't say much when I arrived was not because they were not interested, they were scared into submission to say much.

We finished the day and I achieved the outcomes Chris was hoping to achieve, although I don't think we moved the needle as much in the organisation as was possible. Chris and I went to the bar after the workshop and we debriefed. He asked me for next steps in terms of helping with the culture. I let him know that in order for the business to change, he had to change. The team needed to have a say and to feel valued for their contribution, he had to be more open and more exposed.

He didn't like the sound of that, no surprise.

Trust is the Glue of Team Culture

If you want a well-oiled sales team and to hold onto your talent, then trust inside the team is the key to longevity.

There should be trust between team members so that they can support and jump in to help when required and trust between you and the team.

David Horsager, a friend and Hall of Fame speaker in the USA wrote a wonderful book on trust: The Trust Edge.

David identified eight pillars of trust that were found to be present in all good teams which he coins the eight Cs of trust:

Clarity: people trust the clear and mistrust the ambiguous

Compassion: people put faith in those who care beyond themselves

Character: people notice those who do what's right over what's easy

Competency: confidence in those who stay fresh, relevant, and capable

Commitment: people believe in those who stand through adversity

Connection: people want to follow, buy from, and be around friends

Contribution: people immediately respond to results

Consistency: people love to see the little things done consistently

David's work is world's best practice and he knows trust.

Think about it for a moment, how many of these C's of trust are present in your organisation? Are you clear in communicating the vision and goals of the sales function of the business?

How about compassion?

Do you show enough empathy when the sales team is working hard but not breaking through?

Do you keep the course and not choose the easy way out of reducing expectations when you know the team is capable of achieving the numbers? Are you constantly *sharpening the saw* in the team so they can keep fresh, playing the long game and not falling into the working hard frame of mind all the time?

And how about the big challenge of sales leadership: consistency? Are you getting the team to provide performance that doesn't lead to a big month followed by performance hangover?

Common Values

It all starts with the values of the organisation.

Getting alignment from sales, marketing, operations, warehouse, and customer service takes time in the process. Sales traditionally will bring in "competition and achievement" as core values and others may have "service, commitment, and loyalty" as their values.

Common values that I see in sales teams and then in the "single enterprise" conversations with other departments are:

- Competitive
- Trust
- Respect
- Reliability
- Integrity
- Loyalty
- Honesty
- Commitment
- Efficiency
- Care
- Compassion
- Fun
- Passion
- Perseverance
- Service
- Teamwork
- Clarity

There are a number of others I could have listed, but these are the more common ones I see when I run workshops with cross-functional teams. In terms of your direct sales team, what values do you believe they would share with you if you were to do this exercise?

Try it and find out. I have found that if you have done a fair amount of behavioural style work with your team their answers will reflect what you know about their style.

A more dominant or behavioural style will tend to pick "competitive" or something more "results oriented". The more people focused style like an amiable will choose things more like "relationships or trust."

Choose from both sides of the room and then get agreement to the values of the sales team. Once we have values aligned, we can then move forward.

Agreed Behaviours

Targeting those behaviours that are representative of the values above are fundamental to making sure we all understand what the definition of those values are.

If we are talking about "competitive" as being a value we live by, then we need to create a behaviour that reflects this such as converting business or being the best team in the industry.

You might create, say, three to four agreed behaviours behind each value and then document them.

These can be used internally on documents between the departments, on a scorecard, or perhaps they can even be visible to the team on the wall with posters. (I have seen a few of those in my time.)

The secret here is to create a list that the team can relate to, let them come from the floor so they own them. The more specific the examples they bring up at this point, the better the conversation.

Just watch out for dirty laundry, this is not meant to be an opportunity to score points from each other.

Measures of Success

So how will you measure success of these agreed behaviours to make sure we are living the values? Sales results measures are generally pretty straight forward to get from the team for these behaviours. I have listed many of these in the section on performance standards.

The challenge here is in quantifying other behaviours to make sure they cascade down—a value like "teamwork" or "trust" is more challenging. Going deep with the team, asking them to measure that behaviour—this is your role in creating an agreed culture environment.

Feedback

Many evolved sales teams that I have observed believe in the value of the 360 degree feedback surveys where both sales manager and sales team provide honest feedback on each other's performance.

As long as the frame up of this conversation is right, I can see the value of this process. My caveat here again is that if you have a great communication loop through some of the methods mentioned in the third section, Transformational Coaching; there should be no surprises.

Feedback is critical to the formation of a dynamic sales culture. It says to the team, "Are we on track with what we discussed?"

Agree on how often you will receive feedback. Is it a formal process or very fluent as and when something comes up?

Use sales meetings, one-to-one meetings, quarterly reviews, and company retreats as opportunities to check in on the culture and to see if we are living the values.

Review and Course Correction

So how often will you review your progress on this culture pathway? Is it a monthly process, quarterly, or yearly? I always like to get feedback on progress as soon as possible, especially when you are mapping out a new journey.

Be bold to review and get everyone's real opinion about whether the behaviours are truly accurate of those values you set or whether there is a behaviour that you may have overlooked.

Take a leaf out of the AFL team playbook that requires a debrief at the end of each match where they look at the key numbers that are tracked but then also the "brand" of football they all agreed that they would play on the field—everything is deconstructed. A sales culture should be instantly recognisable to the new inductee to the sales team. Ask them with fresh eyes for what they noticed in the first weeks of their role as a sales professional on your sales team, let them be honest and ask:-

How would you describe our culture here?

You could also go further and ask:-

Did anything surprise you about our culture that you have observed in these first few weeks?

It takes work to stay the course and to honour the direction you have all agreed to—things get in the way and short-term actions become a priority. The "through line" to the sales team is the culture, the fabric of "how we do things around here."

It shouldn't move according to this week's shiny object.

Sales Leadership Transformer: What culture do you want and how will you start the process of discussing it with the team?

CHAPTER 10

Selecting and Creating the Dream Team and the All-Important First 90 Days!

So have you got the "right people in the right slots" to make your sales culture execution a reality?

By the way, most sales teams work the other way around—they already have the people in the team and then they try and tweak the culture rather than leading with their dream of the future and then working back to the personnel they require.

I was doing a sales culture workshop last year with a team and it was obvious within the first 30 minutes of the half day workshop that the team was controlling the sales manager.

I guess you would call that "the tail wagging the dog."

My experience has been when you have a couple of high performers in the team that produce really great numbers, the sales manager gets gun shy about making any changes and doesn't want to rock the boat.

The high performers sensing this then start to dictate the agenda to the sales manager.

We all want high performers, they help us to gain market share and to reach our budgets but they also can also be disruptive. When push comes to shove, you need to decide if you want an environment where the team is stronger than the individual.

One of our real challenges of being the sales leader is walking that fine line; getting the most out of our high performers while also engendering a great team spirit inside the sales team. In the really successful sales teams that I have worked with, there is an understanding that the brand of the company, the sales systems of the company, the marketing of the company, and the client relationships of the company are the things that create company IP and equity.

The sales positions are there to implement the sales plan and to make it happen, to do their role.

Time for some tough love.

As a sales leader, one of your critical roles is to make sure that you stay close to the critical client relationships with those key accounts so you are not "held to ransom" by assertive and ego-driven sales professionals.

Did I really say that?

As I said at the start, this is a book for sales leaders and not sales professionals, a book unlike any other where we tell it as is and not sugar-coat the answers. This is real and goes to building a sales-driven organisation.

In selecting and designing your dream team, our job is to make sure that those who are in the team can do the numbers that are expected of them. This reality is tough as we give people the benefit of the doubt, but for how long?

Sales leadership is all about making the tough calls, to recognise when there may be someone more suited to the team.

When evaluating your current team, ask yourself:

What sales are you potentially missing out on by not having the right people in the right slots?

Think about:

- The wasted leads and opportunities not being converted
- The customers who might not be happy with the person who is calling on them
- The impact on the team of how the person is not performing and "pulling their weight"

- Mistakes being made down the line with the customer service and warehouse functions in the business by misinformation being given
- The promises that may have been made and not kept

I am not saying for a moment that any of these challenges come from people deliberately making your life a challenge. I really do believe that most people who come into the sales team come with the right intentions.

Sometimes it's just "square peg, round hole."

Selecting Your Dream Team

In my coaching work when I work with a sales leader, I look for the following:

- Attitude
- Selling skills
- Product knowledge

You are always looking for all three, however if there is one that is a non-negotiable by a long way, it is **attitude.**

I have always worked on the basis that I can train and coach on the skills I want and others in the company can help me with product knowledge. Attitudes, whether they are positive or negative, can be developed over a lifetime and there may be many environmental factors that we can't change that make it very hard to train them out of it.

A poor attitude, one that is full of ego or arrogance, will weigh heavily on the mood of the sales team.

A negative attitude about a lack of company funded leads has the potential to be infectious.

A positive sales team member will be generous with their fellow salespeople, always open to sharing an idea and can be a great support for you. So many sales managers I have worked with think that if they can hire people just like them, then the team will be unbeatable.

Wrong. Every sales team needs a combination of extroverts and introverts, people-oriented and facts-orientated people.

There are hunters and farmers in every team, those who are really good at bringing in the new piece of business to work on and those who really feel much more comfortable servicing the business and finding the organic opportunities from there.

But then there are also the hybrids.

These salespeople are asked to pivot between creating new business and servicing their portfolio. They are not easy to find. If you have inherited a team from your predecessor, you need to work out quickly whether or not the team you have in front of you will perform at the level you want.

Logically, when there is ground to cover, it is easy to fall into the trap of submitting to the old adage that "someone occupying the chair is better than no one".

Having run my own teams, I can understand the argument. But simply… it is flawed.

Assembling the Team – What to Look For

Think about these things when hiring:

- What is the role we need to fill?
- What are the "non-negotiables" you are looking for in hiring the right candidate?
- What are the "nice to haves"?
- What are the key numbers to fulfil: total sales budget, expectations on new business versus existing business, number of new accounts to be opened in the next 12 months?
- Do you want them to have any experience in your industry? (By the way, the answer is not always yes to that question.)
- What personal attributes are you looking for? (They need to fit into your team.)
- How much of as self-starter do you want versus someone who you are willing to train, sculpt, and invest heavily in?

Write the answers to these things down before you go to market—the problem is that without some key criteria you will compromise all the time with the person in front of you.

Behavioural Styles Can be Helpful

Ken Keis, President of CRG Consulting in Canada, has been a great resource to me in understanding the various style characteristics of people. In 2008, I became accredited in the CRG model of style preference as a licenced partner in Australia and teach their selling style indicator tool.

CRG uses a methodology where the salesperson's preference and potential bias for facts / people; extroversion / introversion; and verbal / non-verbal can be established fairly quickly. I have found the tool to be excellent, and it provides each salesperson an opportunity to grasp the importance of selling style and buying styles of their customers and prospects in my sales training.

The tool is also a great recruiting tool for salespeople.

I would always recommend that it be part of the selection process for every sales leader as it may just give you some insights.

It's not the total answer, but it's a part of the answer.

Hire Slowly, Fire Fast

The late Wayne Berry, head of Top Gun Business Academy and a friend of mine, always said that "if you select in haste, you will repent in leisure."

Sales leaders are always open for business when it comes to

recruitment. There is always talent out there, you just need to be available to accept it.

My dad always said to me, "it costs nothing to talk," so what is lost by meeting with an outstanding candidate even if all the slots are taken? We talk about nurturing the sale with potential customers—why wouldn't the same be true for potential candidates for positions?

Which brings me to firing.

I say to do it fast when you know someone will not work out in the team. The sales numbers are down, the pipeline is not showing a lot of promise, and you are hearing excuse after excuse. These are worrying signs.

When you delay the firing of a sales professional, you are not helping the team and the business thrive:

- The sales team disharmony due to the under- performing sales professional will de-motivate the team.
- The lost opportunities by not having someone else taking over the territory from the under-performing sales professional may end up costing the company money.
- The angst and frustration you will encounter is significant due to procrastinating about the decision.
- The anxiety and sleepless nights you will create by playing it over and over again in your mind will make you unproductive.

- The salesperson will not increase in self-esteem from the whole process as they will each day be wondering when the axe will fall.

The truth is that if your sales processes and accountability systems are in place with each salesperson and the understanding of the rules of the game are made clear during the induction, the salesperson will almost self-select.

Your "Special Sauce" Process to Selection

The screening process for the new candidate should be rigorous and it should involve someone else outside the organisation who is an independent third party. Every time I have played that role for my clients, I have been able to open my clients' eyes.

Use multiple interviews and give the candidate a job to do in preparation for the meeting. If a candidate is not prepared to do a little work prior to turning up, then they don't deserve the opportunity to join the dream team.

Try creating some scenarios to see how they perform; better to get them to do a little bit of work then to hire them and then find out later!

Scenario 1:

Ask them what they know about your company and your competitive advantages in the market. Watch for the genuine attempts at crafting a presentation that requires some research.

Scenario 2:

Give them a challenge and ask them how they would handle it. Perhaps a client challenge or a competitor putting a new product in the market at a far reduced price.

Scenario 3:

Ask them what they would do in the first 90 days in the job. How do they see that being played out in detail?

What do weeks 1 – 13 look like and what would they expect from you and the organisational support?

Scenario 4:

Ask them for their best learning experience as a salesperson in the past. What happened and what did they learn?

Scenario 5:

Ask them something nice and broad and see what comes back. Ask, "What is your selling philosophy?"

Scenario 6:

Ask them for what they believe makes an ideal Sales Culture?

I don't see the hiring process for the new sales professional in the team as being a normal hire inside the company.

Call me biased but the salesperson is a brand ambassador, representative of the company in front of the client as well as the sales professional.

Hunter vs Farmer

Are you looking for the hunter, the farmer or the hybrid?

The attributes of the hunter are very different from the farmer, and I think the candidate in an interview leaves clues as the meeting progresses. We need to ask questions they are not prepared for—look for the language and the facial expressions.

A great client of mine and member of my Sales Leaders Roundtable, Matthew Walton from Symmetry Human Resources, hires salespeople.

I asked him for his "special sauce," the things he really looks for in targeting the right salesperson for the client organisations he works with.

I think he beautifully summed it up: "I look for solid examples of setting and achieving goals in the candidate's life, both in and outside the workplace."

A proven track history, in other words.

Promises can be made in sales, results are real.

As a quick snapshot, here are the main things I am looking for the in the two general types of new hires:

The Hunter:

- A competitiveness and desire to win
- Language about commission structure and OTE (on target earnings)

- Questions around the lead generation philosophy of the business
- Written evidence through their resume about business growth history in previous roles with solid references to verify
- A quiet self-assuredness, not arrogance.

The Farmer:

- A service mindset – a desire to help and develop relationships
- Questions about your team culture
- Discussion around base salary and package inclusions
- Questions around the brand, the company history
- A proactive approach to up-selling, cross-selling, referrals
- An interpersonal behavioural style and length of tenure in previous roles

Square Pegs Don't Go Into Round Holes

When I have consulted to a sales manager in the interviewing process, it is not uncommon for me to remind them that a square peg does not go into a round hole.

In other words, the sales manager has almost "hoped" that the candidate has the attributes and proven track history just because they really liked the candidate.

Perhaps they really wanted to "give them a go" and take a

chance. You can't make a farmer mindset into a hunter mindset overnight, and vice versa. They don't change that easily. One is an autonomous animal who hunts the kill and the other is usually wanting to work as a part of the team and is more service-oriented.

I know this is a gross generalisation, but it has worked for me until now.

Don't get emotionally involved, it will bite you in the backside down the track.

Their References

Proven track record out trumps everything else—not the hope that they can sell, not the qualifications, not the old school tie history, not the presentation.

Interviewing personal references go to character, interviewing business references go to performance. Always look for ways to get better at the art of interviewing business references.

I am expecting their best mate to say nice things about them and speaking to a script when it comes to personal references. However, the business references are richer with information. Ask them things such as:

- Their previous ability to work within the sales team
- Their ability to be autonomous in the field
- Their proven track history of creating new business

- Their personal attributes and qualities
- Their previous performance in self-generating leads and growing a territory
- If they would re-hire them if the opportunity arose

The Cost Per Seat in the Sales Team

Every member of the sales team occupies a seat that could be occupied by another candidate. When you truly understand the total cost per seat in the sales team you can then look at what value multiple you need to create for each sales person. I have worked with sales leaders who really understand this cost of seat concept and others who haven't really grasped the idea.

First, understand all the on-costs of the new hire. Then add to that a formula that takes in a percentage of overhead to be covered. Lastly, add an allowance for an acceptable level of profit.

A great client of mine, Mark Liebach of BusinessCo, a business owner of an organisation that helps their clients with VOIP phone systems, call answering on their behalf, and 1300 numbers, first introduced me to that thinking about 15 years ago. I guess it helped that he was a trained accountant in a previous life and then realised that his competitive personality gave him the skills to drive sales performance of his team.

With this, he had created a formula of what each sales team

member needed to produce in their role in the sales team.

He mentioned to me that there was an expectation of "four to six times salary package" in terms of the sales budget for each salesperson. The multiple now makes the position a profit centre in its own right. I have worked with a number of sales leaders in the past who have their own formulas, whether that be the sales volume of gross margin produced or something else.

Play with a formula that works for you with an emphasis on each sales role paying its way. Now look at it objectively, can the sales people you currently have deliver on that expectation?

The Critical First 90 Days

One of the most common complaints I hear when I help in the recruiting process after the first month or two from the newly hired salesperson is the lack of training and induction in the company. I can see why it happens. When I had my business, I wasn't great at it either. It's only in my consulting to sales teams that I have realised in the last 15 years just how critical to the success of the team it is.

As business owners and sales managers, I think we take a deep breath after the recruitment process and want to get back on with business. The only problem is that we forget to maximise the return on the investment for the new hire.

We may have just spent perhaps in excess of $10k to $20k, depending upon how much of the sales recruitment process we have been involved in, and now we are not making sure we get a great return. Crazy when you think of it!

So it's critical to get the return on investment by making sure we have a rich induction program.

The first 90 days needs to accomplish:

- Solid product training and time spent on the road with someone from the service or the back end of the business.
- Time spent in the warehouse and distribution centre if you sell products. They will learn an enormous amount about how they implement sales instructions.
- Time spent with at least two to three different salespeople from the sales team on the road. They need to see a range of approaches from different personalities.
- Working with marketing to learn about how the value proposition is presented, the collateral is formed, and the challenges they sometimes have with the sales team.

Get Them in the Field Early

I have a contrarian view on the induction of new salespeople from most sales managers. I believe we need to get them out in the field as early as possible with a variety of salespeople to get a feel for the business.

It doesn't matter if they are still undergoing an intensive product knowledge bootcamp internally; they will probably enjoy the time away from it. Get them out.

I have noticed the longer you train the new hire internally, there is a trend to be ready, to be ready, to be ready. In other words, the salesperson will always be making the comment that they need more product knowledge. We don't want them to be procrastinating and to delay client meetings. If they are out meeting clients and prospects early, they can then see how the product knowledge fits with the coal face experience.

The buyer won't be concerned about how much they know initially as long as there is a clear "frame up" of the salesperson's experience and training program they are undertaking from the experienced salesperson at the meeting.

The onus is now on you to be a valuable part of their induction by constantly checking in and asking what their perceptions are. The first 90 days requires you to be an active member of their success. This is golden time for them as they create an impression of what they have signed up to, but it is also a valuable time for you to check in with them to see that their first impressions are as they have fresh eyes.

Sales Leadership Transformer: Do you have the team you want? Chances are there are gaps you know you need to fill with the right fit candidates. "Always be hiring," as we said earlier, but then get active in their success, especially in those all-important first 90 days.

CHAPTER 11

Your Strategic Compass

Sales leadership is all about knowing where you are going and how you will get there. One way of achieving this is through a process I walk through with sales leaders called the strategic compass.

The process allows you to plan for the bigger strategies and tactical implementation plans in your sales team.

Strategy is a core responsibility for the sales leader; it is what we are paid to do. It will:

- Provide a roadmap to where you are going
- Create a direction for the sales team to follow
- Creates a series of priorities to work on in order

So it's now time to develop your own plan of attack in the

market, a compass where you know what you are trying to make happen in your team. Grab a piece of paper and jot down your ideas as they come to your mind under these key headings.

Your Mission

Ask yourself why does the organisation exist? What is the ultimate purpose? Your answer will be linked to the ultimate goal of the business: to provide jobs for those in the business, to provide a good return on time and assets engaged.

What does the business need to do for you? What does it need to do for the staff? Where do you see the sales area of the business within the next three years?

BHAG's

I was first introduced to this concept of Big Hairy Audacious Goals when reading Jim Collins and Jerry Porras book *Built to Last*. They talk about Big Hairy Audacious goals as being "bold missions that highly visionary companies use to stimulate progress."

They quote in their book countless examples of companies who had to be bold over the years to make things happen, to engage the workforce to greatness.

So, where do you need to be bold about setting the direction of the sales team?

Becoming committed to huge, daunting challenges is what

mobilises an idea. I think this applies to sales leadership as well when we set the bar high by stating our bold goal for market share or sales growth.

We limit our thinking in business all the time, mainly because we are scared to fail and perhaps of the repercussions of the decisions we make.

So what if you couldn't fail? What would be the goals you would now set for you, the sales team, and the business? What are the big hairy goals for the business?

In a dealer network, maybe it's to be the "pre-eminent dealer in the network," or to lead a team that's the "biggest in the market with the biggest market share?"

Go on, write something down, something bold for your eyes only at this point.

Don't limit your thinking.

Strategy

What are the ways in which we will achieve our BHAG's for the business?

The strategies are the WHAT of your grand plan.

What are the strategies for the next 12 months that will allow you to have that market share you crave?

Will it require some buy-in from other areas of the business to make it happen?

Tactics

The tactical plan can be broken up into 90-day chunks. This allows you to review progress easily and perform a great number of sales forecasts.

The tactics are the HOW.

It might be, for instance, to…

"…create a marketing program through Facebook adverts for the next 90 days to drive X number of leads."

"…to phone each of our top 20 accounts and ask them for testimonials which we can use in the next corporate marketing campaign."

"…to create a new TV campaign at a particular price point for the new model XYZ."

My dad always taught me to be aware but not "obsessed by your competitors." Guerilla intelligence as a sales leader is useful in aligning your tactics.

Find out what their latest offering is, research their website, and look at their pricing if it's available. It may tell you that you have room to move up!

Get a business associate to shop your competition and find out how the salespeople hold themselves, whether they have a sales process that is well drilled. Get your friend in business to find out where they think their competitive advantage is in the market.

Good to know.

Implementation

This is a list of all those things that would then follow, a series of to-do lists, and there could be a number of these assigned to other sales team members.

These may also be driven by your rules of engagement, the 1 percenters that you have developed with the team around behaviours.

It could be something as simple as a three-rings policy for all incoming calls to be picked up promptly.

Performance Management

Have you created measurement systems that allow you to know at a glance on a scorecard how you are doing towards your goals?

How often will you review the performance of the team and what is your way to set a new strategy if the old one isn't working and getting the results you are looking for?

Do you get the team together and nut out a SWOT occasionally to remind you of where you are strong and what things represent real threats to the industry?

Making Good Strategy Stick

How do we ensure that the strategic compass works in making sure the strategy sticks and gets the results we are looking for?

1. **Focus** – Beware of the bright and shiny objects. Just because your competitors are doing something, doesn't make it right for your business.
2. **Time** – Stay the course with your strategy and not chopping and changing it when you don't get immediate results. Strategy might take years to implement and may not produce results until mid-way through.
3. **Message** – Make sure that the message is clear and not confused with other messages coming out of the management team to the salespeople. An overarching umbrella statement and calling back to that message is paramount for the team to know that you are still working the original plan.
4. **Future-Focused** – Look to the future and not backwards. What is it you see for the future potential for the business? What does the business look like five years from here, and then how do the tactical plans help us to achieve the master plan?
5. **Trackable** – All goals need to have the numbers beside them so you can instantly see how you are progressing. What are your measurables? Do you have a scorecard you have designed that allows you at a glance to see how you are going?

6. **Awareness** – Make sure you keep on top of what the competition is doing. Awareness also means listening to the customer to find out how they feel about the direction you are taking the business. This is a critical role of the sales team to gauge the feel of the market and to report back in.
7. **Congruent** – Are the goals you are setting in sync with the overall goals of the business? There is no point in saying you want a 20 percent increase in number of widgets if the production guys can only produce 7 percent more than last year!

Sales Leadership Transformer: Creating your own strategic compass gives you the ability to recognise what you are aiming for in the long term and then we start to build the plan to make it happen!

CHAPTER 12

The 1-Page Sales Plan—Yours and the Sales Team

Producing a wonderful 30-page document for the board or the CEO or the bank is not the same as producing a great one-page plan that you can use as an implementation of the compass for the sales achievements of the business.

A one-page sales plan... yes, one page.

Many years ago, I was asked to facilitate a sales planning session for a senior executive team. I was fortunate enough to sit in on the strategic business planning session ahead of mine by an expert in strategic planning which focused on the Japanese planning concept of Hoshin Kanri.

It follows a seven-step process in which strategic goals are communicated throughout the organisation and then put into action. The system originated in post-war Japan and was documented as the way that Toyota Motor Company did their strategic planning.

The thing that really caught my attention was the way it starts with the overall plan for the business, then, with a top down approach, it cascades into smaller plans for the heads of each department that make up the overall plan.

I couldn't help but think how many sales plans I had witnessed over the years that didn't have the same level of diligence like this to be successful for sales managers and the sales teams.

The one-page planning process I am about to walk you through keeps this philosophy at front of mind, where there is a process for you to produce your master plan which cascades into the sales professionals individual sales plans.

A great client of mine, Bryan Dance, General Manager of Sales from Nationwide Waste, puts it nicely:

"The one-page sales plan clarifies my goals and business direction in a concise, easy format. It provides a time reference point for course checking."

Without a plan, nothing happens.

You can talk about where you want to get to and dream as

much as you like, but without a sales plan with KPIs and actions, you are just hoping rather than planning for success.

A one-page sales plan will provide you with:

- Key goals for the period of the plan (I am suggesting it is a plan for 12 months)
- Clarity around the key steps required to achieve your overall sales goal
- Alignment between your overall sales goals and the individual sales goals for each of your sales professionals
- A level of accountability in making it happen; if you are constantly referring to it, you now have a document that states what needs to happen and by when.
- A fluid document (I am suggesting it goes into a spreadsheet so you can constantly add and subtract from it as you go along) now it can be updated as you record your progress towards the goals

What Goes Into a One-Page Sales Plan?

Take a look at page 129 and see an example of a one page sales leaders plan.

Your overall sales goal for the plan?

By what date?

The 4 key strategies for the plan that would need to take place in order to achieve the overall sales goals, say:

- Develop your sales dream team
- Create sales management systems and controls
- Motivating the sales team
- Reduce stock inventory by 15%

Now, lets look at that One-Page Sales Plan…

THE 90 DAY SALES LEADER ONE PAGE SALES PLAN

KEY OUTCOME

Sales to increase by $ 1,500,000 from $ 4,500,000 to $ 6,000,000 for the financial year

KEY STRATEGIES

1. Develop the sales "Dream Team"
2. Create sales Management Systems and Controls
3. Motivating the Sales team / Coaching
4. Reduce stock inventory by 15% by the end of the financial year.

KEY TACTICS

Goal Area 1 – Develop the sales Dream Team

Sales person 1 - $ 1,500,000 to $ 1,800,000
Sales person 2 - $ 1,000,000 to $ 1,600,000
Sales person 3 - $ 900,000 to $ 1,300,000
Sales person 4 - $ 1,100,000 to $ 1,300,000

90 Day Actions

1.

2.

3.

Goal Area 2 - Create Sales Management Systems and Controls

To set up accountability expectations

To ridealong with sales people once per month

To develop a 5 steps sales process

90 Day Actions

1.

2.

3.

Goal Area 3 – Motivating the Sale Team / Coaching

Develop a sales meeting agenda and rotate chairing of meeting
Create a 1- 1 coaching process
Create an incentive structure for exceeding budget by min 5%

90 Day Actions

1.

2.

3.

Goal Area 4 – Reduce Stock Inventory by 15% by end of fin year

Run an end of seasons clearance each qtr

To add an incentive for tax time with value add Move stock of 3 yr or more units to wholesaler

90 Day Actions

1.

2.

3.

Four Key Areas of the Plan

Under the strategies, we then cascade down into the key **tactics** to achieve that strategy.

There are **four key areas** to go into the sales leader's plan:

1. The Sales Goals and the Team Members' KPIs

In the sales leader's plan, the individual targets of each sales professional are listed there with the area of coaching for the sales leader to focus on. One of the foundations of the concept is to make sure that when planning at the macro level, you are able to cross-reference exactly how you will achieve this through the individual sales plans.

2. Your Transformational Thinking and Key Projects

What are the key projects you need to commit to as a part of the plan to help achieve the overall key goals of the plan?

Examples of key projects might be:

1. Acquiring the services of an outside lead generation company to produce leads for the team
2. To embark on a sponsorship strategy of key industry associations
3. How about sampling of a new product solution which you want to package up and take to the market?
4. Perhaps developing a new order processing process for

the new sales coordinator position in the sales team

5. Developing new collateral for distribution to clients
6. A new website with a landing page and shopping cart for a product specific offer

3. Your Transformational Processes to Lead the Sales Team

How will you build critical processes that are required by your sales team?

Some examples of these are:

- Your game day sales process for the sales team—from rapport building through to a confirmed order
- Your message to market for all the sales team to follow
- Your sales presentation format to engage stakeholders and executive team when you are pitching for new business
- Your price justification model to justify the spread between your solution and the next competitor
- The individual territory plans for each of the salespeople

4. Your Transformational Coaching Processes

What coaching processes are you going to commit to in your plan? Have you shared this with your sales team to ensure that they keep you accountable to it?

We share these in Section 3 of the book.

Processes such as:

- One-to-one coaching sessions
- The sales meeting format
- The 90-day review
- The ride-along
- Your 90-day induction program

The Sales Professionals One-Page Plan

If we want the sales team to take responsibility for their own numbers and their performance, then preparing their own sales plan is a key part of this.

The key here is to show them the type of planning you want them to put into the plan. Be specific, give them a template, and then ask for a draft.

Each salesperson needs to put in their individual targets and then have a column to track their progress.

Section 1—Their Individual Sales Budget

Each sales professional is to fill out their sales plan and the budget to be achieved.

It will identify:

- Sales to be achieved from current accounts
- Sales required to be achieved from organic growth
- Sales required as new business from new accounts

Section 2—Marketing Effort Required

In this section, have each salesperson make a commitment to what marketing activities they are going to commit to over the planning period:

- Outbound new business activities
- CRM activities to reactivate and drive new business
- Brand ambassador activities to fly the flag for the company (i.e., sponsorship, field days, expos, etc.)

Section 3—Account Management Activities

What do you need to put in place for your expectations of how you want the team to run their account base? How much of their time is to be apportioned to the accounts they already have versus those new accounts they need to acquire?

Have Them List in Their Plans:

- Account reviews to be done and when
- Territory time management plan
- New product solutions they will bundle and market to the existing client base
- New spheres of influence to meet in each account
- Referral opportunities

Section 4—Sharpening the Skills

What skill development are they going to commit to?

Skills such as:

- New referral language and process skills
- Developing a great sales process
- Attending some new sales training
- Learning how to get the most out of the CRM system or LinkedIn

Bottom Up or Top Down?

A question I am often asked is whether or not the sales budget and individual sales plans should be a top down or bottom up approach? A "top down" philosophy is where you tell the sales team what you need to achieve for the year and then make each sales budget for them to equal the overall number.

The other approach which is the "bottom up" philosophy is allowing the sales professionals to individually come up with their own sales budgets and then adding them all up to get to the overall sales budget.

The answer is both.

I always ask sales professionals to develop their own forecast first, whilst at the same time asking the sales leader to develop theirs as well.

It's amazing when you get everyone working on their own budgets just how many times you get individual sales budgets in excess of what you had down for each salesperson.

I have found in my experience that you actually have to reduce individual numbers a little to make it fit into the sales leader's expectation.

It could be because they want to show you that they are bullish in their estimates and they know this is what you want to hear! So now, as the sales leader, you bring together the budgets together and come up with a master plan for the business. Put some work into it. It's not just a straight 5 percent up on previous figures. (I have seen this so many times!)

Go through the previous year's sales results, look at each account, and ask yourself what the growth potential is for that account. What level of prospecting and new business do you want the team to commit to?

Now you have a goal, one which everyone has bought into and now has committed to, not a "best guess" general sales plan where the sales professionals are told what they are to do.

The 12/90 Rule

The term of the plan is important. I don't think as a sales leader today you can plan any further than 12 months with the dynamic of what is happening in the market.

Sure, you should have a future plan which looks out – three to five years, but to get sales team engagement, I think 12 months is plenty. Businesses work in terms of quarters during the year—so consider the benefits of having your sales plans all in alignment with the other departments. So now break the 12 months into your 4 quarters.

The 90-day columns in the sales leader and sales professional plan allows you to synchronise your plan with the 90-day review session I have outlined in Part C where we talk about how to keep the team energized and focused.

Knowing True North

The one-page sales plans for both the sales leader and the sales team are crucial components to knowing what true north is, where you are going, and how you are going to get there.

It provides a level of precision to the sales team efforts when everyone can "drop for 10" and recite clearly their goals and what actions they have committed to in order to achieve them.

Sales Leadership Transformer: The 1 page sales plan creates an alignment in the sales team to the overall sales objective.

PART B
Transformational Processes

Transforming the Sales Team

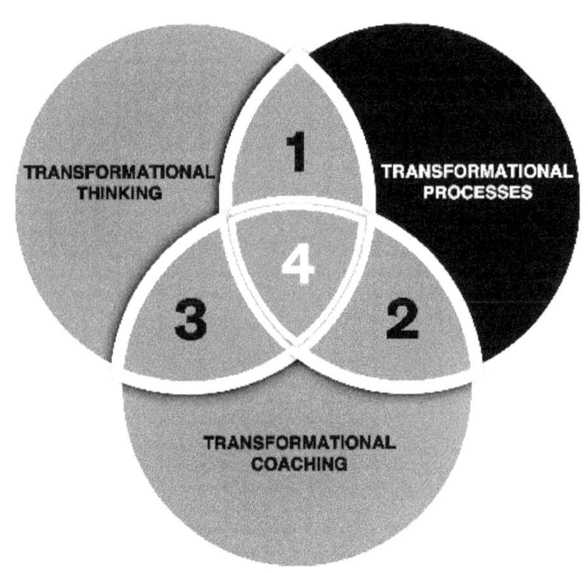

Transforming your Processes gives you a roadmap for success

Most sales managers simply manage activity levels and will be quick to let the team know if they aren't prospecting hard enough or not making enough calls and presentations.

The sales leader looks closely at the sales processes that have a real impact on conversion rates and sales turnover.

The formula to success in sales is activity x effectiveness = results. Therefore, as much effort needs to be put into the effective strategies and tactics to convert more business.

What's the point in having a tired sales team who are frustrated and down on their luck as they are working hard but not getting the results they deserve? Our job is to get into huddles and brainstorm the best way to develop an argument to price, to create a game day sales process, to build language and questions to position us as trusted authorities in the market, and to create flexible solutions.

Sales leadership is not about the blame game and talking behind the backs of the salespeople to other people about the frustrations you have with the team. It's showing them the way to success, to be open to new methods and processes, and to be smart about their selling craft.

CHAPTER 13

The 7 Sales Processes You Must Master to Win!

We quality assure everything else now in business, so why not the sales processes in our team?

There are **seven processes** that, if you can get them right in your team, you will be able to create consistency, accountability, and streamline your road to success.

Process #1 – Your Price Justification Model

In every market, there will always be someone who will offer a product or service cheaper, cheaper, cheaper.

The need for the sales team to able to defend the price differential if you are the premium alternative is a key skill.

We discussed earlier the "value creator" role of the trusted advisor in selling.

When you are selling a premium product in the market you need a strategy to hold margin in the deal. Great language and a comprehensive model helps to cover any "spread" between our offering and a lower priced option. The Price Justification Model is designed to present a compelling argument.

The steps involved are as follows:

Step 1 – Identify a competing brand or business who promotes a cheaper alternative to your solution.

Step 2 – Ask the team and do the research to ascertain the average difference in price between your product and the other alternative.

Step 3 – Now create a model that can be used in every sales call.

Building your model

Level 1 – Tangible Differences

Do an audit and come up with a list of comparisons between your offering and the competitors offering.

Quality of materials used?

Running costs over a period?

Product value at the end of the loan period?

Extra features?

Packaging?

Payment finance options?

Level 2 – Intangible Differences

What else is there in the mix that plays a role in the decision-making process in selecting which offering the customer buys?

Account management services?

Handover process?

Years in the market?

Family owned and operated?

Customer service culture and speed of response?

Take a piece of paper or get started on the whiteboard.

In creating the model, you will need to make a best guess on the numbers. As long as they can be substantiated and evidence ready to go in a selling situation, that's fine.

Set it out as follows:

Approximate difference in price (between your product and competing product)	$ ……..
Less tangible differences	$ …….
Less intangible differences	$ ………
Net difference	$ ………

We can then coach the team to sell the difference and divide it over a number of years or months to get a smaller amount per month.

Level 3 – Evidence Supporting the Business Case

It's time to gather the evidence that backs up our claim as a premium product. Are you able to show models, collateral, case studies, or testimonials to make your case even more compelling? In some industries there has been research done as an industry that supports your argument.

Process #2 – Your Nurture Sequence

Sales teams use LinkedIn as a medium to connect with select new buyers, but there is very rarely any thought put into how we communicate with these prospective buyers beyond the first connection point.

Ever notice the salespeople who, after connecting with you, have the auto-response of a long-winded spiel about how we can work together and let's jump on a call?

Too soon! As my dad would say, "they are asking us to get married before we have been on the first date!" A nurture sequence allows us to take the prospect on a journey with us, to give them a sneak peek at our content and solution.

Consider some of the possible steps in nurturing the lead:-

- An initial email with an introduction after a networking function
- Then sending a special report or ebook that you know will be interesting to them

- Perhaps an article of interest you saw online
- An invitation to a seminar, event, or webinar someone else is running
- How about an invitation to a breakfast, morning tea, or cocktail night you might be running?
- An initial sales call to fact find and establish needs
- A sample order to get the ball rolling so you can prove your great delivery system

Process #3 – Sales Force Automation

I know it's hard to believe, but even today I am finding companies who have little sales database automation in their business.

In fact it's not unusual for me to see salespeople with leads and incoming opportunities scribbled on sticky notes or in the back of diaries. The problem is that the data in its raw form never makes it to the company database as an incoming lead, regardless of whether the prospect becomes a customer or not.

Any future opportunity to cross-market another new product or to consolidate the record into the automated email campaigns is gone and the future conversion opportunity is wasted forever.

Some businesses with silo thinking will have records over different systems, it is departmental and not centralized as a marketing and sales tool for the whole of the business.

The customer and prospect database are a part of the unique intellectual property of the company. When I sold my business back in 2008, this is what got me 90 percent of the total sale price of the business. Whether it be Salesforce, Infusionsoft, Zoho, or a string of others out there, there is a cloud-based solution waiting for you right now. Good CRM (customer relationship management software) allows the team to be able to talk with the customers with confidence about their ordering patterns, their previous quotes, and those matters outstanding.

Your sales force automation must provide the sales team with:

- Access to cumulative sales turnover by account
- All outstanding quotes currently on the system that need follow up
- Call cycle information—those who have been visited and those who still need to be visited if on a regular call cycle
- Fulfilled and unfulfilled orders
- Key contact records on each account
- Lead tracking and qualifying
- Proposal preparation
- Order entry

- Pricing schedules
- Inventory checking
- Expense reporting
- Progress on monthly and yearly budget
- Gross margin tracking

What non-negotiables do you need to put in place to ensure that the entry of important data is made into the system?

Process #4 – The Sales Pipeline

One of the biggest challenges sales managers have is to get their salespeople to prove the reality of where their sales are going to come from. They check in with their sales team by asking, "How's your pipeline?"

Answer: "Really good, I've got 33 opportunities right now worth $2.5 million."

And the sales manager goes, "Last week you had 33 opportunities worth $2.5 million! What's changed? How many of those are real?"

Answer: "I'm optimistic."

That sounds like a dream, not a plan.

My message is: *get real!*

A weekly pipeline report is critical to the monitoring of the performance towards your desired results.

Making the sales team accountable to keeping this updated

is our first job as a sales leader. Then following through and making this the control document for progress made is just as important.

A pipeline can be simply a company name, the contact name, a date, the product they have been quoted, and the estimated value of that piece of business. Or you can really make it hum by pre-determining stages of the sales process and have that as a part of the report.

For example, these may be the stages of the new sale being made in your sales team with each buyer:

- Identifying opportunity
- First meeting
- Follow up to the first meeting
- Presentation of the proposal
- Follow up
- Confirmed sale or business lost

You can make this as elaborate as you like, it depends upon whether the sale is one that is made on the one-call process or whether a typical new piece of business takes multiple presentations over a longer period.

What you are trying to ascertain is whether there is enough activity in each person's pipeline at the current conversion rate to fulfil their budgetary needs. Now be strategic. I have been in sales meetings where the pipeline reports for each salesperson have been methodically line-by-line been picked over (I wouldn't recommend it if you want them to all be awake at the end of it).

Simply pick out those entries you want to ask follow up on and making it public at the meeting. Remember, our objective here is to not embarrass or belittle anyone.

It's simply to let the salespeople know that you are across all the information and you would like an update.

Process #5 – Your Game Day Process

Formalising your game day sales process allows you to structure a process that works and you can tweak to improve.

There are five reasons as to why having a great sales process that the team can follow is important:

To create consistency in your sales team

I was always taught from a young age in sales to come out of the sales call on a new prospect and ask yourself, "What three things could I have done better?"

Leave a professional impression on your buyer

We want our team to be memorable.

Save you time and the time of the buyer

Time is critical in the mind of the buyer, but it's also important for us to maximize our weekly activity.

To recognize where you are at all times so you can constantly improve

When you know your process, you can plan what to bring on the call and how to craft the presentation.

Allows you to role play and rehearse

Get input from the team at sales meetings as you brainstorm new methods. A great sales process will take your buyer on a journey of discovery. It will leave them feeling important and it always creates a logical next step. Specifically, have the **sales process** bullet pointed with the following headings:

- Preparation for the sales call
- The key questions you want answered on a discovery call
- Your message to market
- A list of objections and the answers to each one
- Suggested ways to get confirmation of the business
- Handling the paperwork for the sale made and expectations of what is required

Four Core Drivers of Buyers

Buyers are motivated to purchase for many reasons.

Salespeople should identify them and appeal to them. Understanding the thing that drives the person (can be more than one thing, by the way) will make a massive difference to the conversion rate in the end.

A friend and mentor, Jim Pancero CPAE, renowned sales speaker from the USA, and I were working together on a program in Dallas Texas in 2010. We brainstormed together four core drivers that we identified motivated the business-to-business commercial buyer to buy.

If you can train your team to speak to these drivers when the buyer is giving signals as to what is their dominant buying motive is, they will convert more business.

Make My Life Easier

These people want it done for them. Price is not an issue.

"Just make sure your product is easy to buy and easy to handle" is all these customers want. They are just as likely to hand over a credit card and say "charge it" if they are convinced you will take valuable hours away from them.

Lower My Costs and Increase My Profits

How does your solution help them lower the cost to the prospect's organisation?

Can you replace a fixed cost with a variable cost? Can you increase their sales and profits?

Lower My Risk

Analytical buyers want their risks lowered. They will be attracted if you find a way that reduces a risk in going ahead.

Social proof, testimonials, third-party endorsements, quality assured, cognitive buying… these are all ways to lower risk.

Increase My Competitive Advantage

These buyers want to know that using your product or service increases their advantage over competitors. Exclusivity is one way of doing this.

Selling Skills

In developing your game day process, what are the **selling skills** required today of our sales team in front of the prospect?

Here are some that I always look for:

- To be able to present the product or service with passion
- To be able to convert all product features into key benefit statements
- To be able to create a sense of urgency in advancing the sale
- To have clear steps in the sales process with a method behind each step
- To engage the prospect or customer with theatre
- Match what the buyer is saying to you with one of the four core drivers
- To be able to ask great questions that gets the buyer talking and to be provocative to gain attention

- To be able to deal with all typical objections you get consistently with a flow
- To be able to confirm the business
- To provide three ways to get a YES response

Process #6 – Your Referrals Process

What is your expectation for your team in creating referrals and trusted introductions? I ask in my workshops, "How much of the time do you ask for referrals and introductions from your clients?"

The average response is "less than 25 percent of the time." If you ask, "Why," the answer comes down to:

- Never been shown how
- Don't want to appear too pushy
- Don't want to ruin the client relationship

I don't think this is unusual. We are typically not good at doing it here in Australia. It's not in our makeup to ask the question, and yet if we have done great work with clients, we have earned the right.

Referrals are zero cost leads, and the good news is that a qualified referral will always convert at a higher rate than any other lead. Do you let clients know that you are always in the business for more business?

Bill Cates, a great friend and colleague in the USA, known

as "The Referral Coach," talks about developing referral seeds in the conversation with a client. A seed might be, "Don't keep me a secret," or, "I always have room for more," or perhaps, "I would love to be of service to your business associates."

How do you want them to approach clients to gain trusted introductions?

How about as a company and sales team? Do you need to pay some attention to a company referral program?

Eight Steps to a Great Company Referral Program

Step One: Don't call it a referral program.

Change the language. When you have your salespeople tell your clients about the referral program, they will run a mile! Try "Client Appreciation Program."

Step Two: What is your end game?

What are you trying to achieve? Are you trying to keep clients longer, get a flow of new prospects, or are you trying to get a bigger slice of the pie? It could be all three.

Step Three: What is your current rate of referral?

If you haven't already monitored it, trace back your last six months and work out where your clients came from.

Step Four: What are you willing to give in order to get?

What is a new client worth to you? You may be surprised when you total the spend over a period of five years or more.

This gives a strong indication of how much you can afford to invest to get new business.

Step Five: Create a program.

Produce a flyer, starting with a "thank you for being a client." Arrange a client appreciation day when you get together with them for an evening of drinks, nibbles and a guest speaker. Or maybe a workshop where your CEO says a few words about what's new.

Step Six: Bring your plan to life.

Most people offer 10 percent off the next purchase, which is a good offer but it has no zing. Think about what things would appeal to your customer base? A dinner for two? A CD? A DVD? A night at the opera?

Step Seven: Build the script for the salespeople.

Here is some language you might use:

"We find a number of clients become like part of the family, and as such, we like to reward them for the help they give us in building our business."

"We have recognised that the easiest way for us to build our business is through our loyal happy customers and this is the reason for our client appreciation program."

Step Eight: Keep score.

What response are you getting from all the above? Which

of your incentives are resonating with your clients? If you are cross-selling other parts of your business to the referrer, are they repeat-buying?

Process #7 – The Competitor Matrix

Regular shopping of your competition just makes sense and is a great way to keep current with what's being offered in the market. The competitor matrix allows you and your team to be at the forefront of what is being offered in your industry.

Competitor intelligence is valuable:

- To understand any price premium you are asking
- To keep the sales team informed as to what is being offered
- To be armed for when a customer queries what the competitors have shown them in a presentation
- To see if there is a process or service they are offering that you are missing in your offerings that you need to add

A competitor matrix is a simple multiple-quadrant diagram that you can fill in when comparing a competitor's offering to yours. It may include:

- Pricing
- Inclusions
- Features of the products
- Service guarantees

Sales Leadership Transformer: Create processes for success. Your role is to lead the team in how to sharpen the saw so they convert at a high level.

CHAPTER 14

Setting Performance Standards and Explicit Instruction

I mentioned earlier that we assume a great deal in sales management. As a sales leader, setting performance standards and making instructions clear is a key to success in implementing your sales strategy.

Explicit instruction is all about creating clear expectations of process and deliverables, whilst the performance standards are mutually agreeable by you and your team.

Let's start with setting the performance standards.

Performance Standards

Some of the most common metrics I brainstorm with sales

leaders in developing the performance standards are:

- Sales volume $ and % increase
- Margins achieved
- Activity rates of new proposals
- Conversion rates of new business won
- Average piece of new business in dollar value
- Retention rates of existing accounts
- Budget versus actual of marketing budget spend
- Turnaround timing of orders
- Sales of bundles and new product lines
- Overall organic growth rates per account

Some of the other performance standards we instil, but are much more difficult to measure (although still critical to maintaining the standard) are:

- Contribution to team and willingness to pitch in
- Overall professionalism
- Brand ambassadorship
- Reporting of data
- Compliance of paperwork and systems

Figures are figures and are a great deal easier to set and then keep salespeople accountable.

But what happens when the numbers are slow this month, this is where it is prudent to have other standards of excellence.

Setting the Standards and Your Scorecard

The standard is the standard.

Not saying, "It's okay," when a standard is not met is also part of your journey as well. We may not want to offend, to upset the most experienced of the team, but that's not the point.

I have found that these standards fall down for a few reasons in a sales team: they were not made clear in the outset, there was no clear agreement by each salesperson, and generally a "near enough is good enough" sort of position if the sales target has been reached for the month.

Like the coach of the AFL team, if you are looking for moving the needle on behaviours and creating the new team standards of excellence, then the results should follow.

I guess you could call them the 1 percenters.

Create a scorecard and list the measurements you are putting in place with the team, and then make this the fabric of things that are reported at the sales meeting, rather than some of the administrivia.

The scorecard could be a visual representation that is displayed as a PowerPoint, I have seen many which are printed charts and scorecards where it is easy to identify if we are on target or not.

Explicit Instruction

There is a function of the sales leader that the sales manager is not always quick to take on: the teacher.

Not all sales managers also make good teachers.

But... if you expect your team to be good at a skill, such as getting referrals, positioning the company during a customer sales call, doing an account review, or holding a product demonstration in front of the customer, are you prepared to show them exactly without any doubt what you expect?

This is where we are back to assumption again: *"They will just know."* Clarity is king in sales leadership, right down to the key steps in completing a task like CRM database entry and updating of customer enquiry, etc.

Explicit instruction means getting amongst the team and showing them exactly what you are looking for. If you want them to do a product demonstration, lead by example first and show them how to point out all the features and benefits of the product or service.

Great sales teams first get a thorough briefing, perhaps in an induction, but then things are not followed through and we don't continue to put the chocks behind the wheel. We need to provide "how-to steps" as the sales teacher and then back it up with video-based learning for all processes so the sales team can review at a moment's notice.

It's all about taking away any excuses for not knowing the process, to have the sales team focused on driving the activity and effectiveness goals. Time pressures and other conflicting priorities will always be a reason for not doing what needs to be done. Things that are immediate then become urgent.

Role playing is something that is grossly underestimated in setting the standard.

Salespeople in most teams coming to my training will hate the idea of any type of exercise where they are expected to sit in a hotseat in front of the room to learn a new process or skill.

I always ask for volunteers in my training and it's always a fun, positive learning experience where my goal is to make sure the person learns something upfront and also feels like a success by imparting knowledge with the team.

As a salesperson, it can be the most rewarding experience as you are forced to learn fast and to apply the example the sales leader has given immediately.

Video-Based Instruction

Rather than reinventing the wheel all the time with having to do explicit instruction with all new recruits and to refresh experienced salespeople, why not put down a number of those training and induction processes on video and make it available on the company intranet? There are plenty of processes that can sit there and be accessed by the whole team:

- The history of the company and products/services
- How the manufacturing process works
- Your expectation on how to prepare for a sales call
- The message to market with your key competitive advantages
- How to prepare the quotation or proposal
- Writing up the sales order
- How to process the order with customer service
- How to prepare the shipping instructions
- Filling out the credit application form and the use of personal guarantees

Over the years, I have been asked by a number of clients to produce a set of videos on the back of my training under copyright so they can be made available to all new salespeople in the network.

These were skill–based, such as rapport building, questioning techniques, sales process, messaging, presenting skills, objection handling, confirming skills, etc.

The benefit of this is the saving of time for the sales managers at various locations, but it also means that all salespeople can already be up to speed with my training before I deliver the next series.

The Sales Playbook

Reinventing the wheel is a common fallacy of sales teams that I have worked with over the years. Sales letters get rewritten, database instructions get repeated, and induction programs are hit and miss.

There has been a significant amount of time and money put into developing these processes and now is the time to make sure we have them all in soft and hard copy form so we can tweak and improve on them as we go along.

The Sales Playbook allows us to create a process, flesh it out with steps and expectations, and then document the process so that it remains the intellectual property of the sales team.

The Sales Playbook process can really make the induction of new salespeople a proactive one that has a structure to it so you don't have to go around in circles. Use the playbook and previously discussed video instruction as the foundations to your in-house company training program.

The Sales Playbook is a central source of "how we do things around here" as a sales team.

Here are the components I design when I'm with a sales team:

- Your vision, mission, and BHAGs for the team
- Your message to market
- Your Price Justification Model showing how you can

sell against a low-cost competitor with the specifications list, etc., for more technical products

- Your game day sales process
- Your scripting around outbound new business calls
- Your pipeline report format
- Your quarterly sales report format
- A number of questions that could be asked in each phase of a face-to-face meeting
- The competitor matrix mentioned in the last chapter
- Profiles of each salesperson and key department managers to attach to proposals
- Language to use in the sales process
- List of not-negotiables of the sales team
- Proposal format with a simple edit function so that the proposal can be customised to each client

Let the mind get creative and also ask each salesperson what things they think would be of great help to them.

Soft and/or Hard Copy

Pick your own method. I always like to have a physical folder and then add to and subtract from it while also having the soft copies on the system. Do both.

A binder allows me to flick quickly to find things, especially if it is all tabulated.

It's easy to add articles of interest, printed fliers, and copies of standard forms they can access while the scanned versions and PDFs may be on the system. PDFs of documents and accessible docu-sign type documents that the sales team can use when they need to get client signoff can be kept in folders on the system and simply updated. Perhaps remote salespeople can access the forms by Dropbox or a similar program.

The Bottom Line: Consistency and Clarity

One of the great frustrations of sales managers I meet is the lack of consistency in their sales teams.

They feel that they are being taken on a roller coaster ride of results and effort rather than a more "steady as it goes" mindset.

We set down these expectations in sales leadership, but we don't always provide the tools to achieve. A playbook creates a "way we do things around here" and a structure for success. It doesn't have to be cast in stone, just a fluid process that allows you to tweak as you go.

So where do you need to make the performance standards you have set collectively clear and to reinforce the message to the team? Do you need to go back a step or two and invent some processes now so you can save big amounts of time in the future?

Sales Leadership Transformer: Be explicit in your instruction and don't assume anything!

CHAPTER 15

Creating Your Message to Market

Knowing your competitive advantage, even if it's a slight advantage in a competitive market, will give you a way to mount an argument and build your case.

It's a minimum standard moving forward for salespeople who want to succeed in the next decade and beyond.

Your buyers may already have a vendor that they are very happy with. Why should they switch to you? What is it about you that makes you different from the others? And why should your buyer even consider your proposition?

Jim Pancero CPAE, a good friend of mine and hall of fame speaker in the USA and I worked together in delivering agricultural selling programs.

Jim has a saying:

"The number one question in the buyer's mind is, 'Out of all the vendors available to me – why should I buy from you?'"

He and I brainstormed a process that answers this question and all sales teams must be able to duplicate to make themselves well positioned to sell their competitive advantage.

Your answer could be, "Because my product is unique." But your product is NOT completely unique, that's the truth of it.

The answer to the question, "Why should I buy from you?" involves a planned response. It requires a dramatic realisation of your core message.

Now it's time for a well-rehearsed yet seemingly "just thought of it" message to market. A one-line statement as an umbrella statement and also a longer explanation about what makes you different to create a compelling argument.

I began by saying there is nothing unique about your product and I'm going to contradict myself by claiming that everything about you and your product is unique when used in combination.

But… does the buyer really value what you value?

Of course, it's a great qualifier also really. If you are giving your message of uniqueness to a potential buyer and they are not seeing value in what you are presenting to them about your point of difference, it will help to determine that you are not the right person for them but equally that they are not the ideal customer for you.

Remember, the art of great selling is to make sure we talk with the right type of buyer and not just anyone with a "heartbeat and a wallet."

It also requires us to capture people's attention with a soundbite that creates an immediate connection.

Say you're a diary publisher like I was many years ago before selling the business in 2008. There's nothing inherently unique about that in some ways. Debden, Day-timer, Collins, and Filofax all published day-books or organisers.

All of them have daily pages, expense envelopes, and weekly planners. They all have $16 diaries and a range of up to a couple of hundred dollars. The unique element is what is conjured.

Our brand **NGT** started from humble beginnings, a family-owned business. We had the same products, a variation on a theme.

So when the products are so similar, how do you then come up with something that separates you?

What could that be? Ease of purchase? A local office? Special treatment? Product knowledge? Faster? More helpful?

I had to keep coming up with points of difference.

What we found in that business was that the features of the

product were never as important as the **delivery guarantee** we gave with our products.

Corporate customers could not afford to get their diaries and planners late each year. The reality was that they were used to send out to their best customers and usually were customised with their logo on the front cover. It was a reflection of their promise they had made to their customers.

We knew if we were to "guarantee delivery of their product on time or their money back," it would stick, as our industry was littered by corporates who were disappointed with broken promises of late delivery of product out of China.

Here's another example of idealisation. How about services and selling ideas and concepts in the market?

Some years ago, I hired a well-known speaker who taught a daily session about "Nine Types of Difficult People."

He had reduced all the problem people in the world to nine types. Why nine? Why not 11? Why not 27? Answer: it was nine because he said so.

That's all it was.

Why Have One Message?

So, why have a prepared message of uniqueness you can recite and deliver to any existing or new client in the market?

I think there are plenty of reasons:

1. **To increase** the professionalism of your selling process and to position you as a true trusted advisor
2. **To create** a consistency across the sales team or enterprise
   There is nothing more impressive than when a sales team can individually recite their message of uniqueness to customers across the counter or on a business-to-business sales call.
3. To **hold margin** in the sale
   The marketplace is as competitive as ever and the buyer knows which buttons to press to get what they want. Your message to market creates a compelling reason why your company or brand and your reputation are strong enough to command a premium price in the market.
4. To remind good customers why they shouldn't consider a **"low-ball offer"**
   By introducing your message of uniqueness into your buyer conversations or account review agenda or testimonials, it puts doubt in the mind of the buyer when entertaining moves from a competitor who wants to cut the price to acquire a new client.
5. **To increase** your self-esteem and confidence in the negotiation process

A good deal of sales success in salespeople comes from keeping a fragile confidence in check and self-doubt under control. By repeating the message of uniqueness on every sales call, it really sells you on why you do what you do and bulletproofs your mojo.

Bringing together a message requires brainstorming, finessing, and then market testing with the whole team being in on the process and the benefits of it.

Let's take a look at the key components:

1. The Umbrella Statement

A one-line statement—a soundbite—that you can use anywhere in a meeting that makes you and your solution unique.

An example might be:

"We work with **(target market)**, to **(what outcome?)**, through our **(process)**."

So if I was to be delivering my own message to a sales director or small business owner, it might sound something like this:

"I work with salespeople, sales managers, and business owners to increase conversion of leads by implementation of my Trusted Advisor selling method."

2. The Four Core Drivers

We discussed the four core drivers of our commercial buyers in a previous chapter.

They were:

Make my life easier

Lower my costs or increase my profits

Lower my risk

Increase my competitive advantage

At this part of the message of uniqueness, we are feeding back to the buyer the driver(s) that we think we have heard in the sales call and using that language back in the conversation.

Pick out one or two to use.

3. The Three Core Reasons

The best messages are simple and contain three main messages that make us different, and no more.

When developing this with your team, ask them to brainstorm all the reasons why someone should buy from your company.

Some of the popular reasons are:

Our expertise

Our extensive product range

Our superior customer service

Our years of experience

Family-owned for over 30 years

Our dealer backup and network

Our old-fashioned values and "we care"

Our customised solution

And… much, much more.

4. Evidence Statements

Once you have developed your main reasons, or pillars as I like to call them, it is now time to back these up with real evidence.

The evidence might be presented in the form of something visual, statistics, or models.

Things like:

Product demonstration

Key industry data

Price Justification Model

Client testimonials

Process visuals or models

Collateral or brochures

Website

Personal anecdotes

Are you able to back up your uniqueness statement with evidence and a compelling argument that makes the buyer salivate at the idea of working with you?

The buyer has a decision to make: stay with the incumbent, a low-risk decision where they get what they know even if it's not perfect, or take a chance and go out on a limb with this new entity and to give them a chance.

Most conservative buyers will stay with the former unless there is a real reason to change, a mistake or series of mistakes by the incumbent or perhaps a price advantage.

In a bid situation where you are asked to pitch for the new business, either one-to-one or one-to-many in a board or management team opportunity, your ability to come up with a succinct rationale for using your business is critically important.

Delivery of the Message

The last part of the theatre of the message to market is in the delivery of the message. You never want to appear that the answer is rehearsed and rote learned, even though in reality you have used the same message in every sales call.

The use of a pause, providing time to reflect while the question is being asked, all adds to the theatre and the suspense of the answer. I always preface the answer with something like—

"If I had to think about it, a few things come to mind as to what separates us in the market…" and then I start to articulate a few key things. You also don't have to "press play" when giving the answer; it doesn't need to be perfect.

So what happens if you are never asked the exact question—"Why out of all the vendors available to me should I buy from you?"

That's okay, that's where real theatre come in. Simply ask the question of yourself in front of the buyer and then answer it. Impressive.

Your buyer will be super impressed you know succinctly the answer to that question. This is worth rehearsing and getting it right. The application of this process is that it allows you to consistently tell the same story in your verbal presentations and also in your written word in proposals and copy.

When building this with your team, write your answers on a pad, flesh them out, and ask the team to keep it with them when they hit the road for a sales meeting.

Reverse Engineering

The power of the message of uniqueness comes from talking in terms the buyer's interests and not what you want to brag on about. One method I have found to be really effective in building your message to market is to ask your customer. Doesn't sound that hard really does it? But we don't do it. Ask your customers why they use you and what they most value from your relationship with them.

A method I found really works for me is to tell the buyer

you are working on your website or putting together a piece of collateral which is 100% true as that work never stops, and you would like their help for a moment.

"Would you mind telling me what you find the most important part of our business relationship to be and why you use my services?"

Your current customers will tell you some really important things in answer to the question if you ask them.

Sit back and listen, then go back to the office and rework it. This is designed to be a dynamic process, one where there is no magic answer but what comes from trial and error. Then, when you have it in draft form, go to the final stage.

The bottom line is that we all have preconceived ideas as to what the customer values. When you think about it, the person who should be centre stage is the customer, so ask them!

Many years ago, when I started in consulting business, I was designing my own message. I had a number of things down ready to discuss with the customer and see how they would register with them.

I asked one of my clients if I could enlist their help. I asked them for their feedback.

They replied to me: "I really enjoy all of your material and I know the team gets a lot of benefit from it, but what I value more than anything else is my ability to get your opinion on things. You are my Trusted Advisor! I guess a sort of sounding board before I go ahead with any important sales decision."

Trusted Advisor Selling was born off the back of that one conversation.

How to Use Your Strategic Message of Uniqueness

This process is not just for the face-to-face sales call where we are presenting our credibility to multiple decision makers around the boardroom table. When you have designed it with your team, adapt it to these environments:

The New Business Conversation

Your first appointment is a moment of truth. There is theatre in how you present your ideas and make your points.

The message of uniqueness(MOU) can be used in the rapport building segment or casually at the urn in making a cuppa with the buyer.

You can also segue into the message by making a more obvious frame up.

"Well, I guess I should tell you a little about our company and how we work with our clients."

Existing Customer Review

Whether that be on a regular 90-day cycle or an annual review of performance and reflection on previous business volume, the MOU can be used to reinforce your value to the buyer.

"As you know, our positioning has always been to..."

Meet and Greet Networking

Using a soundbite from your message of uniqueness to position yourself in 10 seconds is a key to creating a great first impression.

At our Friday School of Sales, I ask everyone to introduce themselves in 10 seconds or less as good practice of being able to sell your message quickly to a group of strangers.

After a while of regularly attending, it's amazing how succinct members can get at doing this.

Written Emails/Confirmation Emails

When you are reconfirming the points from your meeting or confirming discussions in a summary email, there is an opportunity to bring in a pillar of uniqueness and evidence statement into the email as an opportunity to restate your value.

Sales Leadership Transformer: The message of uniqueness is a fluid process. It never stops being enhanced and tweaked according to what you are hearing from your customers. Make a start and get the team assembled; create an environment where all answers are accepted without judgement and then build from there.

CHAPTER 16

Creating Your Rainmaking Machine

If there is one mantra I hear often from sales teams as being critical to their success, it's "more leads, more leads, more leads." There are order takers, there are order makers, and there are order creators. The market doesn't pay anywhere near the same amount for each of these roles in a sales team.

The **order taker** expects all the leads to be generated by the company and will be at the total mercy of a solid lead generation machine behind them to achieve their budget, if they have one.

The **order maker** may look for the referral opportunities in different areas of the client relationship and organic growth in the account.

The **order creator** makes something out of nothing.

They are resourceful salespeople who have proven ways of generating leads beyond what is given to them.

They network, they jump on the phones and talk to people, and they ask a lot of questions as to how things operate in the industry when new to the business.

When developing your lead generating rainmaking machine, the first thing to decide is what your philosophy is about how much you are going to feed the team versus the team feeding themselves.

Once you have established that, you can then start to design a system which will deliver to the hungry sales team.

Start to reverse engineer by looking at the converted sales you need at the order value you need them at and then work back to the number of leads required each week or month.

The Best Hunters Can Feed Themselves

Being a "self-generator" is a skill you will pay handsomely for as a sales leader when searching to fill your team.

Anyone can sit in the office and wait for the next email or phone lead to come across their desk.

However, those who can create something out of nothing, to circulate and look for opportunities all the time, are worth their weight in gold.

In a team of hunters, demand that the team generate 50 percent of their own opportunities. I have certainly been in sales environments where that number can fluctuate from 25 percent to 80 percent depending upon the sales culture, and that there are no excuses why that's not possible.

But you must give them ideas and tools, and brainstorm with the team the full range of rainmaking options as you help with them to develop a plan. A trusted advisor sales team will develop a pipeline of opportunities from the following streams of leads. Our job as a sales leader is to invest in providing marketing support and a framework about how they should go about their method to maximise results:

1. Quality Referrals and Trusted Introductions

Two or three new referrals every month would make a massive difference to your business if you, as a salesperson, succeeded in turning them into clients.

This is the gold standard of opportunity conversion as the referrer is directly connecting you with the prospective buyer rather than just giving you a name and number.

Key Success Factor: Doing great work and building trust with your valued customers by reminding them this is how you create almost all new clients.

2. LinkedIn

In terms of business-to-business social selling, this medium is head-and-shoulders above everything else. The key success factor is consistency. I think LinkedIn has become a game changer simply because when I started out in selling and had a decision maker move on from a company, you would always wonder where they went. With LinkedIn, that person remains a contact for you and you even get a reminder from LinkedIn that the person has started with a new company. You can then send a message and congratulate them!

Key Success Factor: Connect with them, nurture them, and ultimately move them out of LinkedIn and onto your email list.

3. Webinars

Online webinars give out information and should always issue a call for action at the close.

But they are more than that.... they help to introduce people to what you do as a sampler and provide a reminder of your value to existing clients.

Your strategy should be to create a low entry point, then see if they want to continue the conversation through an offer to ultimately ascend up the ladder to become a high value client.

Key Success Factor: Ascension is the key, getting people from the webinar to the next stage.

4. Invitation Marketing

Invitation marketing means speaking at events. If the local networking group or Chamber of Commerce asks you to speak, there might be 30 business owners in the group, which offers you a great opportunity to connect with your target market.

The "work" happens at the backend, like phoning attendees after the event to see if they want to be involved with something else you're doing.

You may also choose to run a number of events of your own: a monthly breakfast or a big annual event yourself.

I run my annual "Great Sales Summit" and we have over 100 members come along, as well as monthly breakfasts near the Melbourne CBD which then deepens into a membership in my Institute.

Key Success Factor: Have something to say, then create a compelling offer... then follow them up.

5. Direct Mail

Direct mail was big in the '80s and I believe it still works.

When you compare it with the low cost of email marketing, the secret is to make sure the direct mail is highly targeted.

It can create a sense of urgency when packaged in yellow Express Post envelopes.

People will always open an Express Post mailing. It's about curiosity.

To be cost effective, the envelope has to cut through.

Spend the money on getting a professionally written letter to go in the pack, add your promo inside, and then send out a number each week with a follow-up phone call.

Key Success Factor: Send a lumpy envelope and make a phone follow-up within 48 hours.

6. Networking

The key is to get in front of quality buyers. Spheres of influence is about having conversations with a small group of business people who know people or have a scale to their business.

There are networking groups all around the country where you can turn up and enjoy a light breakfast, coffee, and conversation directed to actively generating lead-swaps.

We are aiming for a couple of quality conversations with the right people. Befriend the organiser and ask who is who when you arrive!

Key Success Factor: Be able to have highly targeted strategic conversations and get involved to help. Arrive first and leave last.

7. Telemarketing

There's still a place for telemarketing. Set aside two to three hours per week. You might even employ someone to do your calls. Start with current clients, try lapsed clients next, then those who have been quoted, and work your way down to colder introductory calls because they are the hardest. Telemarketing is another numbers game. I attend many "boiler room sessions" where highly motivated salespeople assign, say, a two-hour slot each week to all jump on the phones together and make calls. It creates a mojo boost each week, and as a sales leader, this is about driving a proactive culture.

Key Success Factor: Build a database of hot, warm or lukewarm buyers, then commit to a time and day for it.

8. Facebook Ads

Facebook and LinkedIn ads are part of the way we monetise the social media activity. Create a social media strategy and buy the expertise. You will have hit-and-miss success, but it's a way to keep your brand name out there. Make it part of your activity to regularly post content on all social media platforms, but control the expectation of the sales team as it can be one of the most bright and shiny objects where salespeople get lost in feeds and forget what their job is: to sell.

Key Success Factor: Commit to the medium. Don't expect a sharp increase in sales. It takes time with posting and developing regular content.

9. Email Campaigns

Develop your email database. This is ultimately yours and a big part of the business goodwill. Give good content. Tag your subject line well so it doesn't shoot straight to junk before being read. Consider that your recipient may be getting 30-60 junk emails when they open their computer, so yours has to stand out. A catchphrase that has curiosity value is important—say something like—"Try this" or, "You will want to read this."

Key Success Factor: Balance your communication just right between promoting offers and delivering great content ideas and strategies people can use. It will make sure the open rates are maximised.

10. SMS

SMS campaigns direct to the customer's phone is an excellent reminder of current arrangements. That's their best use. Asking them to confirm yes/no is the simplest use.

Dental and medical practices do it all the time. I notice many service providers use it also for an offer which will close before a certain date.

Recently, it has also become very popular with the motor vehicle industry in making their database aware of a sale that is happening.

Key Success Factor: Don't try to do all the selling on an SMS, use it to announce something or remind them of something.

Create your rainmaking plan

Lead the team with developing a rainmaking plan that creates opportunities inside the team to convert more business.

Challenge them to be resourceful, there is a joint accountability here where the business provides resources and they bring sweat equity to the table. There is nothing worse than having a flat sales team sitting in the office waiting for a lead to arrive by chance. Drive a scorecard that is mutually agreed to by all parties and forms part of your one to one conversations.

In your one-page plan mentioned earlier, go to the section of "marketing projects" and make a commitment to ongoing activities: meet with experts in lead generation, SEO, and social media, and create a program that works.

Sales Leadership Transformer: Rainmaking is a core function to the success of a great sales team. As the sales leader, help create a plan with the team of expectations and then make sure you keep up your end of the bargain in terms of marketing activities.

PART C
Transformational Coaching

Transforming the Sales Team

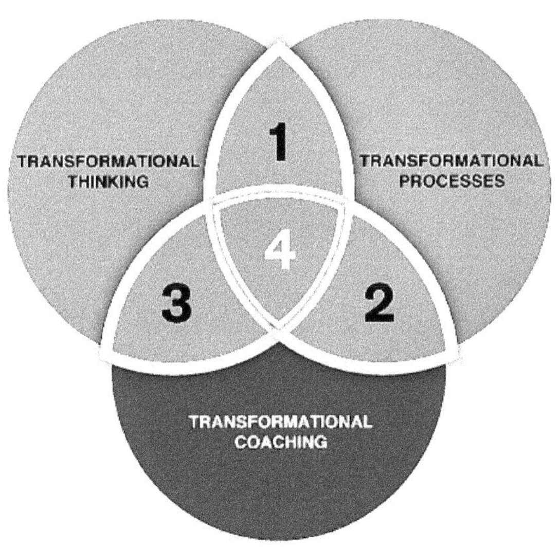

Why Coaching is a Key Part of Being an Effective Sales Leader

Coaching is all about how to create high performance results through the sales team by being there as a coach and mentor.

Our role is to nurture talent, to be a positive influence, and to be an "unreasonable friend" when they need to have challenges and excuses called out.

We are looking for changes to the sales team in their:

- Mindset
- Attitude
- Skills
- Application and effort
- Results

Our role is to coach them so they see the need for new skills. We then facilitate the extra knowledge they need and then get them to apply the knowledge to create a sharpening of the skills, and then to have a thirst for more.

Celebrating the wins and the success with the team is fundamental to creating the type of atmosphere and culture you want to create. Coaching also means knowing your behavioural style and their style and how you encourage higher performance by talking the language that works for them.

So let's start on this coaching journey with a few initial questions to see how you rate yourself as a coach.

1. Do you talk about your mistakes before pulling up your sales team all the time?
2. Do you ask questions rather than giving direct orders all the time?
3. Do you praise in public and correct behaviour in private?
4. Do you throw down a challenge to each member of the team to encourage higher performance?
5. Do you tailor make your coaching according to the individual salesperson?

CHAPTER 17

The Things That Motivate Salespeople and Paying Them What They are Worth!

There is one belief system that says you can't motivate salespeople; they must motivate themselves as it comes from within. I don't disagree with that, but I think you can certainly ignite the flame that creates the action to get them moving.

The interesting thing is that it's like the AFL football coach: you need to know what buttons to press to get top performance from a star performer.

I was interviewing a great client of mine, Martin Bates from Stow Australia, on my NewSelling program and he spoke about how he motivates the team.

"Money is the obvious one but working just as hard on smaller prizes that can provide a small motivator in a competitive sales team is important. Whether that be the weekend away package, the TV set or even the gold class movie vouchers with the meal package included.

"It's amazing how $200 spent can create enormous competitive spirit inside the team."

So what motivates salespeople?

Well, it depends upon their style and makeup.

Here is a list of those things that have always worked for me in getting enthusiastic cooperation from the sales team:

Money

Well, the obvious one.

It's not everything to the sales team, but it's the easiest to co-ordinate and the easiest one to quantify.

You have plenty of choices here—it starts with the base package and it needs to be competitive.

It then needs to have plenty of "blue sky" or upside, salespeople are built this way. Again, I have been surprised over the years how many sales managers have not had an incentive for salespeople to earn more.

Money also means bonuses: monthly, quarterly, yearly. When they hit a milestone, they should be able to get more.

The secret is to make that bonus level a stretch but not out of their reach—that will have the opposite effect.

It can be a spot bonus based on sales of a certain package or even a number of a certain product sold over a single day or week.

Security

If you are a more introverted style, you may be a little risk averse. A number of technical salespeople I have worked with over the years are of this style. They want to know that they will still have a job. It's your job not to scare them and place them under unnecessary pressure to play for their survival.

It doesn't mean that you allow for mediocrity in performance, but don't lead with the possibility of them losing their job.

I know when I sold my business in 2008, the first concern from the customer service and admin team was whether they would still have a job. When we negotiated the sale with the buyer, we put in a condition about keeping jobs, and of course they had to assure all staff that their superannuation and long-service entitlements were all taken care of.

Recognition and Acceptance from Others

Everyone wants to be recognized for their contribution to the sales team, but some crave it more than others. Making reference to a member of the sales team at the sales meeting and the effort that they have gone to in that week will go far.

Salesperson of the week, month, or year boards are common place in large sales teams. They work. I remember when I consulted in the telecommunications sector there were always breakfasts put on for the best performers throughout the state and then throughout the country.

In the trucking industry, they have a top dealers group and also an elite group for the top 20 salespeople around the country which includes a trip either locally or overseas.

Consider a mounted plaque that is presented at the monthly company get-together or even a morning tea celebrating any salesperson achieving 25 percent above their budget for that quarter or year. Nothing better than having to present a number of these. You would be surprised by the impact of a good plaque.

Achievement

Certificates on the wall go a long way in a sales team. For some, it's also being able to print onto their cards "Senior Sales Consultant" rather than just sales consultant.

I know the real estate industry is clever with this. LJ Hooker has always had the "Captains Club" logo on the business cards of its top performers around the country.

In my early 20s, I was once a trainer for Dale Carnegie Training in teaching the Human Relations and Public speaking course. You may know the work of Dale Carnegie from his best-selling book *How to Win Friends and Influence People.*

When I was training to become an instructor, there was a process at the end of that training when you were awarded your instructor pin and a letter personally signed from the head of instruction at the New York City head office.

I still have that certificate framed in a pride of place in my office. It is one of my most prized possessions.

I have been involved with a sales team in the pharmaceutical industry where the highest performer on the team got to claim the spare car spot for the month and they even went to the extent of getting a small plate made up with the person's name on it. It might sound small time, but I can tell you I genuinely observed a desire to hold onto that spot for the next months by keeping the numbers up and not having to give the spot back.

Self-Acceptance and Self-Esteem

Just touching back on the Dale Carnegie course I mentioned earlier, Carnegie's book talks about not criticizing, condemning, or complaining. It also talks about giving honest, sincere appreciation and showing an interest in others, all priceless human relations principles.

I have met a number of salespeople with low self-esteem. Sounds contradictory to what people think of the salespersons personality, but take a salesperson out of the bravado of a sales meeting and you find out what is under the surface.

Salespeople, in my experience, need to maintain a strong self-esteem and self-acceptance to know that they can be successful in sales. Our job is to believe in their ability, to encourage, and to not be personal in our critique of process or results but to talk to the fundamentals.

Just them knowing that you believe in them and letting them know they can do it if they put their mind to it will go a long way. When they are having a hard time, remind of them of what they are capable of when they are selling at their best. Be their coach, their mentor if they need it, and remember what impact you can have on their enjoyment of their work.

Think back as a salesperson, think of the great mentors in your life, the people who believed in your ability to deliver for the company. I have been lucky to have many along the way who knew I could to it, even when I had doubts myself.

Paying Them What They are Worth!

A contributing factor to how your sales team will sell is based on how they are compensated.

As an "employer of choice" brand in the market, think about how you want others to see the compensation program of the business. It needs to be attractive enough to get people engaged and to make the recruitment process easier.

In constructing your compensation program, first think of what level of compensation a candidate would expect to earn if they were about on target with their budget. When we talk about the package to lure a great, high calibre salesperson, the number you need to lead with is **OTE – on target earnings.** It's a very important number as the best salespeople are not thinking about the base package. This is only to make sure all the basic needs are being met. The best ones are thinking how they can reach for the sky and be a top performer.

The next step is to work out what the right level of base pay is and what the "at risk" performance pay portion should be.

Also think about what non-selling activities you want the salespeople to be involved in. The lower the fixed salary, the less follow up you will generally get from the sales team, unless it's in their interest to do it.

The perfect rule I've always found to follow is asking what level of impact and influence the salesperson had on the new piece of business. If it is self-generated through their own efforts (they have never purchased from us before) then that deserves the maximum success payment I am willing to offer.

Don't Underestimate the Power of OTE!

You live and die by the OTE—make it too low and you won't achieve the best talent, make it too high and you will have a revolving door due to people thinking that the job was falsely represented.

I wish I could have a dollar for each time I have seen a sales manager talk up a job and not really put any work into developing a solid model that reflects the method to achieving the target. Who in your team is currently earning at that level?

This will be important as it provides evidence to the business case. Show any new hire the way in which they can make the OTE and then they will salivate at the opportunity to work for you. How much base and how much commissions and bonuses to get to that level? Is there a right percentage?

Many will argue a higher percentage than me. I think a split of approximately 70/30 works pretty well for their on target earnings. The 70 percent will mean they have their very basic needs all met and can pay all the bills at home, but they still want their 30 percent as that allows them to reach for the stars.

Some sales managers also like to cap earnings. Again, I can't understand that. I was always of the opinion that if someone was making more than me as the business owner, what do I care? More commissions = more sales and more profits for me.

A fully salaried sales team with "no blue sky" will have a

different culture than a 70/30 sales team.

By the same token, a fully commissioned team with advances made against future commissions may have a "dog eat dog" culture as basic needs are not being met at home.

The type of balance you end up with for any new position will serve as a natural filter and qualifier for those people who apply and then continue with the interview process.

Get the Expense Reports All Sorted

I feel like I am getting operational at this point, but I wouldn't mention it if it wasn't a problem in a number of sales teams.

Unrest and frustration on both sides over the simple expense report doesn't make sense to me. Just make it clear, if you are happy for the sales team to stay at a certain hotel, hire a certain car, and fly on a flexible ticket rather than a cheapie, then say so.

If you want them to live within a certain budget for the meal and bar allowance, then say it. The last thing you want on either side is to have a stand up argument about the cost of a beer in the lounge bar.

One last thing, have a policy in place for dinners and entertainment for clients and prospects. If they are trying to bag an elephant and they can get some alone time with the decision maker, is a dinner for two at one of the top restaurants in town a fair investment? You decide.

Enough said with the boring stuff.

Determinants of compensation

A good compensation program will usually take these things into account:

- The type of salesperson you want on the team – one who is going to open doors—what level of follow through do they need to have?
- Balancing your needs as a company and the level of comfort for the salesperson
- The amount of account servicing you are expecting
- The level of paperwork required—or will the sales coordinator do a good deal of the paperwork?
- How much influence the salesperson has on the sale itself or whether the company produces a great proportion of its own leads
- The type of the product or service sold and the price point in the market

Spot Bonuses Can Work Nicely

Perhaps keeping things interesting with some spot bonuses dedicated to a certain product or market would be a good idea. We did it with some of the products we were trying to move from time to time. "Double commissions on this product for the next two weeks or an extra 20 percent commission if you can add this to the sale" is not uncommon. Many salespeople don't look too far beyond the next quarter, so having a short-term bonus for the particular type of sale you are looking for can work well.

I have seen this in motor vehicle sales where there may be a model they want to move quickly, and in telecommunications when a new plan hits the market.

Sales Leadership Transformer: Spend the time to really understand what motivates your team and then make a concerted effort to make the money right. Salespeople need certainty around money—it provides a stake in the ground.

CHAPTER 18

Ride-Alongs

If I had to pick one tool in the toolkit that can add the most value for sales managers transforming into the sales leader and becoming a great coach it would be ride-alongs.

The problem, in my experience coaching and mentoring over 500 sales managers on my journey, is that most don't do them very often at all. If this is new to you, a ride-along is simply a time when you get out in the field with one team member for a one-on-one sales call visit where you can watch and learn from the way they sell in the market.

The payoff is huge. You get to see first-hand what the salesperson is doing when they are in front of the buyer, you get to spend some one-to-one time to understand them individually, and you get the feel of the market.

The other little known payoff is the opportunity to confirm more business. There is no doubt in my mind when you have two minds working on the sale, there is a higher chance that you will find organic opportunities to grow the account or to get a new piece of business signed up!

The sales manager gets involved too late in the selling process. The sales leader is at the front of this process. They get involved in the formulation of a compelling offer, the strategy behind the pitch, and the pricing of the unique packages to give the opportunity every chance.

This is where the ride-along comes into its own, a process that helps you get better at being the strategist and the coach in fine tuning the process.

Create a culture of self-improvement, and include yourself in that conversation. When the team can see that you are transparent enough to let them know that you are a constant learning curve, it changes the dynamic.

Now you have a frame to keep going back to and a reason why the ride-along is important to the sales team. "Our culture is one of constant and never-ending improvement."

To make the ride-along process work, I like to do the following:

- Let the team know that it is part of the sales team

culture to do these regularly.

- Let them know that it is not about checking in on them but it is about working together.
- Give them advance notice so you set them up for success.
- Make it a not negotiable on your part—don't get in the habit of cancelling them

Create the expectation of how many calls, the spacing in between each call, and how the day will run. Don't underplay it and let familiarity take over or you will find it very hard to provide the level of objective coaching that will get the results you are looking for.

It's better as a sales leader to write the day off or at least the morning and let the salespeople know when you will be going out with them, it will allow you to organise your week more effectively.

So, what makes a good ride-along process? The more you put into the set-up, the more you will get out of it. I coach a simple **three-step process** that really gets results for sales leaders.

Step1 – Pre-Call

A briefing in the car with the salesperson or at the desk before you leave for the appointment should only take, say, 15 minutes tops. Define each other's role, work out what would be a good outcome, and discuss the format for the call.

I have found there are certain questions I want to ask to make sure we set the experience up for success and to find out how much preparation the salesperson has put into these calls.

Ask each salesperson at the desk or in the car on the way to the appointment:

"Tell me about this call, who are we meeting with and what do you know about the company?"

If they are a current customer, ask:

"What level of business are we currently doing with the customer?" (even though you would already have a very clear understanding of the answer to this question).

Ask: "What's your outcome for this sales call?"

By the way, it's not the answer you might be thinking. It's not necessarily about having a signed order from the buyer! Your objective might be to get a full audit of their needs, or to find out how entrenched they are with your competitor.

Ask: "How do you want me to play it?"

In other words, you are asking what your role is and how will they introduce you on the sales call.

I have always found as a sales leader of the team that it's an easy position for us to take the "big picture" role, to talk about the company, the history, and to ask strategic questions about their history and growth goals.

Let the salesperson talk about the specifics of the call and the order or potential order. They may already have a great relationship with the contact and it's important for them to keep building on the day to day rapport.

Step 2 – Observations on the Call

So now you are in front of the buyer and you have been introduced and played your role to flag wave and talk big picture about the company.

Be careful here to not be the school teacher, jumping in all the way through the sales call. This is not easy, especially if you can see the sales call going south and not having the right impact! Don't correct the salesperson on the visit unless they say something factually incorrect. It runs the risk of belittling them in front of the buyer.

Watch for those things they are doing well. There is always something to point out in the debrief, but keep one eye on the buyer's face and one eye on the delivery of the message from the salesperson.

Look out for buying signals from the buyer and don't be

afraid to politely jump in if you can see that the salesperson is missing some positive signals.

Many years ago, I was coaching a young lady on a sales team at a telecommunications company I was doing some consulting work with in the western suburbs of Sydney. Rebecca seemed well prepared and was going back to deliver to the proposal in the hope of securing the mobile phone contract. It was a great opportunity, about 100 mobile phone connections.

She handed over the proposal and starting to go through each page starting with the background of their company and the history of their ownership. She then moved on to the next page which was discussing their current usage and current provider, etc. She had done her research.

The only problem was that she wasn't keeping one eye on the buyer and they had now moved over to page 13 which was the summary of the dollar differences between the current plan and what she was proposing.

The buyer then got the calculator out and started to make calculations on the notepad beside them adding up the potential savings across to the fleet of mobile phones.

I'll never forget the appointment as the buyer's name was Brad as well. I couldn't help myself. I jumped in and asked: "Before coming here today, what was your bottom line to this changeover?

In other words, what was your expectation of how much money you would save by going with Rebecca's proposal?"

He answered back: "About $1,000 per month is what we wanted to achieve."

I then asked Rebecca what the savings were. She answered, "$910 per month."

I jumped in: "So, do you think you can make that happen with the stakeholders?"

He replied: "Yes, I think that will be fine."

Rebecca was still back on page 7 now drawing attention to the phones and the options available—just close the business!

The debrief was invaluable to her. She didn't even realize that the buying signal was so loud and would have totally missed the opportunity to confirm the business were it not for the ride-along.

Make some mental notes, or if you have to note a few key words in your journal, that's fine as well. Observe and note what you like and where an area of improvement could be.

Look for process, language used, questions they could ask next time, and the way they developed rapport with the buyer.

I asked my good friend and terrific client Dave Ballantyne, General Manager of ISUZU NZ, what he looks for in sales managers and salespeople in the network.

He really sums it up well:

"One of the key attributes I am looking for in salespeople and sales managers is having the ability to engage with people effectively and build a relationship from the start.

You can have all the technical ability in the world, but it won't mean much if people are not comfortable or reluctant to enter into and build a relationship with you. I guess that's reflected in your approach of becoming the trusted advisor."

On the ride-along you are looking for the technical ability but you are also looking for the way they interact with each buyer. You can't get a sense for this working behind the desk, only at the coalface.

Step 3 – The Debrief

Now it's time to deliver the message like a great coach. The salesperson will more often be nervous about receiving the feedback; it's only natural. Make it easy for them, or they won't want to do it again. Frame it up with a conversation about what you like and then move into the areas of improvement.

Use the opportunity on the way back if you are doing the debrief in the car to find out more about them—where they are at in terms of their mindset and what they need help with. Reaffirm their importance to the team.

Ask questions such as these:

"What did you think you did well on the call today?"

"Was there anything that surprised you about the situation, the buyer, or their response?"

"If you had your time again, what would you have changed on the call?"

"What can I do for you as your sales manager?"

This is the time to be the coach and to open up the lines of communication; it's golden time.

Look for opportunities to get agreement on where the team could improve a process or develop a new one.

Now it's time to create an action plan. The ride-along is of little value if you don't create a way forward. Confirm with them as to what you need to do from here and what you can get them to commit to from here.

I always find this process works well when I can transfer the lessons from the ride-along back into the sales meeting. I start with the "spotlight" method (talking and debriefing on the improvements in the car).

Next is the "floodlight" method where we take the conversation to the rest of the team, and you make a feature of the call, what you learned from that salesperson, and what we could all learn. At the sales meeting, you can see the great pride in their performance as the salesperson now recites lessons to the team as to how they go about their craft. Gold!

The Virtual Sales Ride-Along

I think we will see more and more blended selling in the future—the blend between face-to-face selling and the virtual sales presentation. So why not embrace the new selling environment as one that allows for you to coach the ride-along process remotely by being on the virtual sales call together?

Set up in advance the conversation with the salesperson about the objectives of the Zoom virtual sales call. Then have the salesperson invite you into the meeting and play your role.

At the end of the meeting, when the virtual sales call is finished with the prospect, have a separate meeting with the salesperson to discuss next steps for the proposal and also allow time for the coaching session debrief.

This type of sales ride-along is efficient with time and very effective—it will enable you to learn a lot about the salesperson and their preparedness for the call by asking a few strategic questions virtually before the meeting starts.

How seriously do they take this process? How much preparation do they do on their sales calls? How much do they know about their customers and prospects?

These are all questions you will have a much better grip on by making a real commitment to the ride-along process.

Sales Leadership Transformer: Invest in the team and quality assure the sales process by committing to ride-alongs. Develop your process around these 3 steps and it will then provide an important part of the personal development of each sales person.

CHAPTER 19

The Sales Meeting

If you are not having a regular sales meeting every week, you are missing a golden opportunity to provide some important direction to the team that really gets results.

I am amazed at the number of sales managers who overlook this crucial part of sales leadership. The response from so many I coach is, "I try to, but sometimes I just run out of time."

Make time. I am serious, make it a high priority.

The problem with most sales meetings is that they have become a habit rather than a valuable part of sales leadership. The other thing is that most of them are just plain boring.

Trust me, I've attended plenty of them as an observer and coach to sales managers, and I have to stop myself from falling asleep! Perhaps my own sales meetings back 18 years ago were putting people to sleep as well!

When I had my own sales team in the stationery business many years ago, it was hard making it interesting each week. I made the fatal mistake I think most sales managers make—why does it all have to come back on me to bring it together and why do I have to do all the work?

Well, lesson one is that you don't.

Share the load and get the team involved is the moral of the story, more about that in a minute. So let's start with looking at why are sales meetings so important to a sales team.

A great weekly sales meeting:

- Helps to build and maintain a great sales culture
- Gets the team focused for the week ahead
- Allows you to provide a message that sticks once per week with everyone there to hear it
- Can be critical to impart information—although some information is better sent out through other means (we will get to that)
- Allows you to create a single enterprise with members of other departments so they can understand your challenges and the sales team can understand their challenges
- Allows you to rev up the team they are underperforming

- Creates a spark in the team to achieve
- Allows you to train, role play, and impart ideas, strategies, and skills to the team
- Gives you the ability to lay praise on individuals by using the spotlight/floodlight method of feedback from the ride-alongs you have attended during the week
- Gives you an opportunity to map out your master plan—your strategies for success
- Gives you an opportunity to brainstorm an idea and get feedback
- Allows you to update product or solution information and pricing updates

Convinced yet?

Simply, a well-run sales meeting is a victory march for the team! It is also a key part of the job of a sales leader—to be the leader of the team, to communicate, teach and inspire. Even if you think you can't spare the time from week to week, spare a moment for the rest of the team.

Some sales people like to start the week with an opportunity to get together with their work buddies and begin the week with a meeting that gives them focus.

10 Keys to a Great Sales Meeting

1. *Keep the sales meeting positive.* Remember the love

sandwich to giving feedback: good stuff, then the improvement area, and then the good stuff again.

2. *Start the sales meeting with an affirming comment* from you and finish it the same way. It's the first and last thing that they will most likely remember in any sales meeting and not all the stuff in between.
3. *Never run a sales meeting without an agenda*—this is not a talk fest, it's a tactical meeting aimed at getting the focus of the team to hit the numbers for that week, month, and quarter.
4. *Define the start and end meeting times* and never deviate from the times. Even if you don't finish everything on your list or you have to delete an item, you cannot be going over by 30–40 minutes to complete the list. The sales team will lose respect for the process, and if they are doing their job well, they should be wanting to fly out of the meeting to go to their first sales appointment.
5. *Cover the most important items first.* You may not get through everything, so you want to make sure you get the main things dealt with first.
6. *Make sure you give the salespeople jobs to do*: run a brainstorm on getting agreement to the sale, run a session on how they prepare for the sales call, or run a

session on how to develop a price justification model in front of the buyer to protect margin.

7. *Make sure everyone gets a say.* Don't let one or two dominate the discussion. Let's face it, most salespeople love to talk!
8. *Don't give floor time to intensely negative talk* in the sales meeting as it will hijack the purpose of the meeting. Be careful you don't agree with negative talk from the salespeople, and that also goes for any negative comments made of other departments. Take any negative stuff offline and deal with it in the individual one-to-ones.
9. *Best times for a sales meeting are Monday or Tuesday first thing* at say, 7.30 – 8.30 a.m. Add some fun to it by changing the venue occasionally and add in some coffee and danishes or muffins for prompt attendees.
10. *Pass around the chairing of the meeting function* amongst the team. As long as there is a detailed agenda, anyone should be able to run the meeting, share the load.

The Virtual Sales Meeting

In the age of remote sales teams, be even more creative in how you manage the performance of the team and communicate valuable information each week.

Remember when we started this chapter and talked about the reasons for the sales meeting that we made the point that the sales meeting is also about gaining commitment, making sure the energy is right in the team, and providing the mojo boost that salespeople get from being at the meeting.

Virtual sales teams with autonomous salespeople working in the field and from home need the interaction with their fellow team members. Setting up the virtual meeting via Zoom or other methods is critical. Put some non-negotiables in place to make it a successful experience, such as video must always be on, clear agenda emailed in advance, and sharing the screen when you need to distribute information.

All the other rules apply as they do in a live sales meeting—start and finish times, etc.

Future-Focused and Not in the Past!

I think where a lot of sales meetings get off track is the focus on what has already happened. We can't do much about that, only learn from it for the future. How much of your communication is about an expectation that wasn't met, stock that wasn't sold, processes that were not followed?

Sales leaders who are trying to shape the next sales period are conscious of creating a conversation that is future–focused:

your goal for the next month or quarter ahead or a problem that you have foreseen into the future and want to make sure that we proactively get the jump on it.

The sales team needs to be reminded of how they can close the gap on the sales budgets and not told over and over again when they don't make it.

Spend some time doing projections. Break the larger target down into bite-sized chunks and spread the love with some things that are being done well.

Not Minutes – Actions

I have always felt the most important thing about a sales meeting is to get agreement from the team for a pathway forward. You have done all the hard work to create the right environment, to have the meeting hum along, and now it's time for some clear actions and commitments.

Make sure that you get an email out to the team within the same day as to what has been committed to what and by when.

Follow up prior to the sales meeting making sure that people have done their work prior to the meeting. Set your previous meeting and the future meeting up for success.

You don't need that level of formality of minutes —a short action list that keeps everyone accountable will do the trick.

Speed is the key.

As you are forming the list in front of them at the end of the meeting, make sure you get acknowledgement of the actions they are committing to. Make sure there is no ambiguity as to what is expected and then get an email out.

Create the Loop

Your meeting action plan goes out to the team directly after the meeting and should include simple action steps, who is responsible, and by when. This is the document you begin the next meeting with – bring it out and check to see who has done what. Note to self: Make sure you always look at the list and complete your actions before the meeting or you are going to shoot your credibility!

Once you have done this once or twice, watch the level of attention you will get from everyone as they scramble to make sure they have completed their assigned items on the list.

As an early mentor sales manager said to me when I started to run sales meetings: "You want them a little uncomfortable when they enter the room, it keeps the meeting focused!"

Sales meetings are more than a habitual meeting where we all just get together. They are an opportunity to re-affirm the team commitment, to set a forward plan, to remind the team of the big picture, and there is only one person who can do that: the sales leader.

Sales Leadership Transformer: Enjoy the sales meeting and look forward to it. It is a weekly opportunity for you to put your stamp on the team and the direction of the business.

CHAPTER 20

The One-to-One Coaching Session

The Sales Management Association (USA) surveyed American member businesses and found that 77 percent of firms in the survey said "they don't provide enough coaching to their salespeople."

No great surprise there—the question is, why?

We get caught up in busy time, we don't make a high priority of it, and we assume that everyone knows what they are doing! The best sales leaders meet with their salespeople regularly in a one-to-one session.

Even though it seems we have so many other things to juggle at the same time, we can't make it less than a number one priority.

We talked about how our job is to work through our salespeople to achieve the desired results we have for our sales team. The only way to achieve this is for us to be the coach of the team and to take a committed interest.

So how long and how often?

The best sales leaders I have worked with usually work to a timeframe of about 20-30 minutes, that's all. The frequency of about once per fortnight seems to be about right. I have had sales leaders run them every week after a sales meeting to get the focus for the week. That's all okay as well.

What are the benefits of well-run one-to-one coaching session?

- You can maintain the message previously delivered to the team.
- You can spotlight on personal improvements where you don't want to embarrass them in the sales meeting.
- You can course correct when you can see that the salesperson is off track with the tactical plan of the team strategy.
- You can learn a little more about each salesperson and uncover any personal issues they may be having that are impacting their role.
- You can determine much more quickly if the salesperson is or is not going to be a fit for the team and make the

appropriate decisions.

- You can help to reinforce the sense of achievement as the focus is on what has been done.
- The sales meeting becomes increasingly about strategy, high level tactics, and skills and not about reporting each week with the use of coaching sessions.

That's not a bad start.

If we bring together the idea of "forming your dream team" from the earlier chapter with an emphasis on recruitment and holding on to great talent, doesn't one to one coaching make a good deal of sense to get the maximum return on your investment of talent?

Here are **the keys** to running a great one-to-one sales coaching culture in your team:

1. **Never say you are "too busy" to have the session.** It sends a shocking message to the team, especially since they have put it into the diary and allowed the time for it. Even if it requires you doing some of your own work after hours, get back the importance of the sales coaching session.
2. **Block out a regular time for coaching sessions.** I used to always run them in blocks, which allowed me to chunk my time for them. I also found I got better and better at them given that I was doing them back to back. You get

into a rhythm and you will be more effective.

3. **Create a structure that works.** You want the sales team prepared, so create your own structure for a session—follow my formula, or add or subtract from it, but have a structure so that the sales team know.
4. **It needs to be a positive growth experience.** This should not be seen as an interrogation to the salespeople. Remember, you want this experience to be a great success. Always be looking for things they are doing well and then add in those things that would be an area of improvement.
5. **Keep to a time frame no matter what!** Be respectful of their time. Don't create a problem for yourself by constantly going over time. Be interested, be involved, and listen.
6. **No interruptions!** Sales managers who believe that the business can't operate a single day without them will constantly leave their phone on and take calls during the session. Don't allow people to interrupt.
7. **Create an action plan.** Every session must start with an action plan as to what we agreed we were going to work on and to finish each session with those things we want to achieve before the next session. Give them a job or two to do, but also make a commitment to do something for

them, and make sure you do it!

The key components of a great session

1. *Review previous session action steps.*

Ask: "How are you proceeding with what we discussed last time?"

2. *Chunk up on the big picture.*

Ask: "So let's check in and see how you are progressing towards your goal."

3. *Talk the numbers and progress made.*

Tell them to bring along to the meeting:

- Their up-to-date pipeline with conversion percentages
- Hot deals they expect to close off in this period
- Previous week's results
- Upcoming calls and expectations / planning done

Ask: "What's next?"

Find out what the next steps will be for each key opportunity as you discuss each part of their one-page plan.

Ask: "And then what…"

The key to great coaching sessions is to keep the conversation future-focused and not to dwell on things that haven't gone well.

Ask: "Who else do you need to meet at that organisation?"

Ask this if you are coaching them to go deeper and create a

contact at the decision maker level.

Ask: "Is this the best use of your time right now?"

Perhaps you need them to see that they are spending too much time on low priority work?

Ask: "What more can I be doing to help you?"

Ask this if you have noticed that you can add value to the conversations that they are having.

Ask: "Can you enlist the help of..."

Ask this if you really want them to use other resources in the company to help get something done.

Hit the positive.

Ask: "What do you think you are doing well at the moment?"

Look for ways to improve.

Ask: "Looking at how you might approach this situation, what is one thing you think you can probably do better?"

Add value and help.

Ask: "What's something you need from me to help you reach your number for this month?"

4. *Recap and crystalise the actions.*

Ask: "So let's recap what we decided are the joint accountabilities that we can both report back at our next session."

Consider a Pre-Printed Form

After a while of conducting these sessions, you will become very skilled at leading the discussion and knowing what is next in the one-to-one coaching session.

There is still real value in making the format for the session unambiguous so people know what to expect.

By having a form and process locked away in your sales playbook that you can use in the session directs the salespeople to filling in the information they need to for the session. Having a structure with some headings also makes sure it goes to time.

The Personal Development Matrix

As a commitment to learning and development, it's a great opportunity to link into the coaching process a simple personal development matrix.

As a sales leader, you are now showing that you are invested in their constant improvement and have professionalized their skill acquisition.

The matrix may contain:

- Skill area they want to work on
- Specific training to be completed
- Date and venue
- Outcomes expected from the training
- Completion date

- Any timing to revisit the goal
- Approval of the manager

Why not get the salesperson to sign it and acknowledge the fact that these are skills they want to develop and the courses for them to commit to? The one-to-one coaching process can fast track the success of the sales team by getting your direction and mentorship at regular intervals.

If we go back to the key motivators of the sales team discussed earlier, there is an inherent need for a number of salespeople to feel they are on a trajectory of achievement and to feel acknowledged. What a great opportunity this process provides.

Sales Leadership Transformer: One on one coaching is key to getting the most out of each team member. You are saying to them "you are important and these sessions matter".

CHAPTER 21

The Quarterly Review

Sales leadership is all about feedback—your sales team wants it and it's your job to deliver it in a positive way.

Don't shy away from it and make it fixed in the diary three months in advance for the quarterly review meeting.

You will already have in place a yearly review which will probably be linked to a financial conversation, whether that be a yearly bonus and the remuneration review. As much as yearly reviews should always be separate to the talk about money, they are intertwined all the time.

The 90-day review works in sync with the 90-day window you have in your sales plan and the sales professional's sales plan. Make them work in sync, it makes sense to everyone and it also cuts your time.

It is a foundational element to making sure that the team stays on course and that you get an early flag from the discussion as to whether they can meet the standard or if this is not a good fit for both you and them.

It also works in tandem with the probationary period any new recruit will have when they are hired. So if recruiting has that expectation, then why not continue the 90-day process on as a regular part of checking in?

I have always thought that the process of holding a yearly review is really just a formality when you are doing regular quarterly reviews. When you think about it, you should know how your salespeople are performing from the other coaching processes already mentioned.

If the key criteria are set out in the outset and then backed up with the coaching processes, the salesperson should almost self-select if they can't see themselves still being a member of the team moving forward.

In my experience, a number of sales managers I have coached have tended to really dislike the time around review time.

I think there are two reasons.

First, they are concerned there may be confrontation in a difference of opinion over their performance, and second, they tie any discussion of money—base salary and bonuses or commissions to the conversation.

The quarterly review meeting doesn't have to be either. Money should be handled at an annual review and the conversation around performance numbers should all be spelt out in advance. Any skills they are needing to improve again should be communicated in the field.

I guess I am making a point over and over again—good consistent communication with your team members will keep the team focused and will ensure you are proactively able to sense any issues. So what are the objectives of this process?

A 90-day review process will:

- Do a temperature check on their level of positivity around the role they are being asked to perform in the business
- Identify how they are proceeding with their quarterly sales targets and cumulative yearly targets
- Create a culture of self-improvement where they commit to new skills they want to develop and how you will help them by coaching them
- Help you to learn more about the salesperson – to find out what makes them tick and where they see themselves going in their life

- Provide you with any red flags in terms of expectations they have from the company and their ability to self-generate business
- Enable you to deliver what is expected by reinforcing the previous message over and over again
- Send a message to the salespeople that you care about them as an employee and also as a person
- To make sure that any yearly review is not full of surprises, as you have uncovered any problems on the way

Preparation for the Quarterly Review

The quarterly review will be a great experience if you can make sure they have prepared as much as you have for the review.

It will maintain a professionalism about it and not drift into familiarity.

Your Preparation:

- Acquaint yourself with their $ output versus expectations
- Check on their performance metrics scorecard
- Review all notes from the coaching sessions
- Role play in your mind the meeting
- What's the message you want to give?

Their Preparation:

Provide a number of questions and tasks you want them to complete prior to meeting. It will increase the importance of the meeting in their eyes.

These could include topics such as:

- New business generated in the last 90 days
- The updated pipeline of outstanding opportunities
- The marketing efforts they have embarked on
- The skills they have been working on
- Any challenges they are currently having
- Their plan for the next 90 days

The Review Process in Detail

There are two fundamental parts of the 90-day review; *qualitative* and *quantitative*. It's not just all about the numbers, it's also a temperature check to see how they are feeling about things.

Qualitative

Ask:

- How do you think you are doing?
- What's the area you are having a challenge with at the moment?
- You set the goal 90 days ago to… [selling skill]. How is

your progress going with that?

- What's a new skill you now want to commit to improving for this next 90 days?
- How would you know at the end of the 90 days if you were successful at the achievement of that goal?
- What do you need from me?
- Where could I add more value for you as a sales manager?

Run through any observations you have made and provide the love sandwich of what is going well and what you would like them to work on.

In the evaluation criteria, consider:-

- Participation in company events and functions
- Selling skills
- Attitude
- Planning and time management skills
- Product knowledge
- Administrative call reports and paperwork
- Use of the sales force automation systems
- Customer service and handling complaints
- Personal characteristics such as appearance, self-confidence, follow up, flexibility, persistence, dependability, and initiative
- Getting along with team members

Quantitative

Review – scorecard of performance metrics

- Number of proposals given
- Conversion rates
- Sales of specific products
- Average order values
- Retention rates
- Referrals
- Organic growth per account
- Gross margins and year-on-year sales
- Pipeline numbers, dollar values
- Service issues and account management follow up
- Expense control of a territory marketing budget

The session then takes place.

Allow about 45 minutes to one hour and then finish with the written record once again of what was agreed to and then send out an email to complete the communication loop.

There may also be a need to follow certain company protocols, liaise with HR to dig deeper. A combination of the ride-along, the sales meeting, the one-to-one coaching process, and the quarterly review together with a solid knowledge of what really motivates each person on your team provides a great feedback loop as a sales leader.

Sales Leadership Transformer: Link this discussion in with your quarterly reflection of the business overall. Business works in quarters so make sure that the team puts the date in the diary and knows it will always take place, now you have created excellent rigour.

Sales Managers are Obsolete but Sales Leaders are Always in Demand

The new sales world is desperate for sales leaders and not sales managers.

Sales managers will tell you what has happened; the sales leader will tell you how they will shape the selling efforts of the business for the future.

The sales manager will make blame their team for the results they are not achieving, the sales leader takes full responsibility for the output of the sales team.

Sales leaders have a plan and recognise when the plan needs a tweak to produce the desired result.

They listen, they observe, and they are flexible with the pathway.

Be a part of the journey and commit to being the sales leader you want to become.

You may just surprise yourself.

Read widely and look outside your industry for inspiration as the answers may not exist there right now.

The three parts to this book—transformational thinking, transformational processes, and transformational coaching—will give you the tools to build on the journey of developing new skills right now.

Try some of them and hit the ground running right now.

As we said before, the great privilege of sales leadership means that we never stop learning. And… never underestimate the impact we have on others' lives.

Sales teams all over the country and around the world are looking right now to their sales leader for the direction and clarity of vision of the future.

I wish you luck with the journey, and reach out if you would like to let me know something that gets results for you, I would love to hear from you at brad@bradtonini.com.

Yours in Sales Leadership,

Brad Tonini

The Trusted Advisor Selling World

Upcoming Events and Offerings

Additional resources & tools to help you convert more sales

Here's how to experience more of the Brad Tonini Trusted Advisor Selling Method:-

Website —www.bradtonini.com

The Monday Morning Mojo—our weekly video program

Weekly sales program – NewSelling

Join our LinkedIn Group – The Trusted Sales Advisor

Brad's Trusted Advisor Selling Institute runs:-

A monthly "Friday School of Sales" breakfast

A number of half and full day programs in the Trusted Advisor Selling Method

Virtual and face to face sales training for your sales team

The Sales Leaders Roundtable – an intensive groups of sales managers and business owners mastermind program

Announcing the Sales Leaders Roundtable

Imagine meeting with your own mentor group of sales leaders strategically planning and acting to increase sales results through your team!

Join 12 only sales leaders with these processes to get results

- Group brainstorming sessions with sales managers content
- 1 -1 sessions targeted and customised for your own sales team growth
- A toolbox of practical and proven sales leaders concepts and action plans
- A confidential environment for sharing of challenges and building strategies
- A total focus on the 3 main functions of sales management

To learn more about this, email brad@bradtonini.com for the next intake.

Some of the topics we will cover ....

- Your dynamic sales culture
- How to create a powerful sales funnel
- How to show the team how to be dealmakers
- How to create your 1 year success plan
- How to create accountabilities and results
- How to create multiple streams of opportunities
- How to create a effective 1-1 coaching process
- How to do effective ride-alongs with sales people
- How to run great sales meetings
- How to think strategically and tactically
- How to create urgency in the team
- How to maximise opportunities with clients
- How to develop your own sales process

"Brad is the master at showing sales managers how to becomes sales leaders. His Roundtable program has given me so much insight into the new skills and strategies to succeed".

Justin Sheppard

Divisional Manager – Gibson Eyewear

www.ingramcontent.com/pod-product-compliance
Ingram Content Group UK Ltd.
Pitfield, Milton Keynes, MK11 3LW, UK
UKHW020144250726
13967UKWH00002B/858